STAFFORDSHIRE

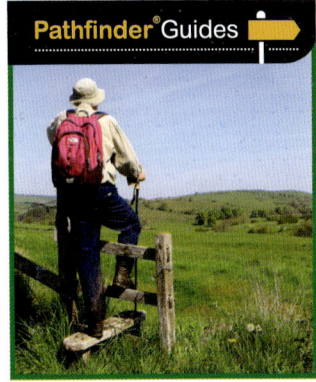

Outstanding Circular Walks

*Compiled by
Dennis and Jan Kelsall*

Contents

At-a-glance	2	Slightly harder walks of 3–4 hours	25
Keymap and Introduction	4	Longer walks of more than 4 hours	75
Short walks under 3 hours	9	Further Information	92

At-a-glance

Walk		Page	🥾	🏠	🚶	⛰	🕐
1	Norbury Junction and the Shroppie	10	A519 north–east of Norbury	SJ 789 242	4¾ miles (7.6km)	245ft (75m)	2¼ hrs
2	Kinver Edge	12	Kinver	SO 845 834	4¼ miles (6.8km)	620ft (190m)	2½ hrs
3	Tittesworth Water	14	Tittesworth Water Park	SJ 993 601	5 miles (8km)	410ft (125m)	2½ hrs
4	Onecote and the Upper Hamps	16	Onecote	SK 049 551	5 miles (8km)	565ft (175m)	2½ hrs
5	Swynnerton Old Park	18	Hanchurch Hills Picnic Site	SJ 839 397	5¾ miles (9.3km)	510ft (155m)	2¾ hrs
6	The Smestow Valley	20	Smestow Valley Nature Reserve	SO 891 999	6 miles (9.7km)	225ft (70m)	2¾ hrs
7	Wheaton Aston	22	Wheaton Aston village car park	SJ 852 126	6 miles (9.7km)	235ft (70m)	2¾ hrs
8	Cheddleton and the Caldon Canal	26	Deep Hayes Country Park	SJ 960 533	5¾ miles (9.3km)	645ft (195m)	3 hrs
9	Rushton Spencer and the Dane Valley	28	Rushton Spencer	SJ 936 624	5¾ miles (9.3km)	660ft (200m)	3 hrs
10	Dimmings Dale and the Churnet Valley	31	Ramblers' Retreat, Dimmings Dale	SK 062 431	5¾ miles (9.3km)	745ft (225m)	3 hrs
11	Cannock Chase and the War Graves	34	Commonwealth War Cemetery	SJ 983 154	6¼ miles (10.1km)	520ft (160m)	3 hrs
12	Fradley Junction	37	Fradley Junction	SK 142 141	6½ miles (10.5km)	140ft (45m)	3 hrs
13	Brewood and Chillington Hall	40	Brewood	SJ 884 088	6½ miles (10.5km)	320ft (100m)	3 hrs
14	Burnt Wood and Blore Heath	42	Loggerheads	SJ 738 358	6½ miles (10.5km)	490ft (150m)	3¼ hrs
15	Three Shire Heads	45	Wildboarclough	SJ 987 698	6¼ miles (10.1km)	1,245ft (380m)	3½ hrs
16	The Roaches	48	The Roaches	SK 004 621	6½ miles (10.5km)	1,180ft (360m)	3½ hrs
17	Dovedale	51	Dovedale Car Park	SK 146 509	6½ miles (10.5km)	1,265ft (385m)	3½ hrs
18	Grindon and the River Hamps	54	Grindon	SK 085 545	6¾ miles (10.9km)	1,025ft (310m)	3½ hrs
19	Milwich and Sandon Park	57	Milwich	SJ 971 323	7¼ miles (11.7km)	550ft (170m)	3½ hrs
20	Ellastone, Calwich and Wootton Park	60	Ellastone	SK 116 434	7¼ miles (11.7km)	730ft (225m)	3½ hrs
21	Gnosall Heath	63	Minor lane, west of Gnosall Heath	SJ 806 201	7½ miles (12.1km)	420ft (130m)	3½ hrs
22	Tutbury, Hanbury and Fauld	66	Tutbury	SK 213 293	7½ miles (12.1km)	490ft (150m)	3½ hrs
23	Froghall and the Churnet Valley	69	Froghall Wharf	SK 027 476	7½ miles (12.1km)	955ft (290m)	3¾ hrs
24	Shugborough Park and Sherbrook Valley	72	Milford Common	SJ 973 210	7¾ miles (12.5km)	770ft (235m)	3¾ hrs
25	Above the Manifold	76	Wetton	SK 109 551	7¾ miles (12.5km)	1,165ft (355m)	4 hrs
26	Kinver & the Staffordshire & Worcestershire Canal	80	Kinver, below Holy Austin Rock	SK 836 836	8 miles (12.9km)	700ft (215m)	4 hrs
27	Mines and Caves of the Manifold	84	Hulme End	SK 103 593	8¾ miles (14.1km)	1,440ft (440m)	5 hrs
28	Wolfscote and Biggin Dales	88	Alstonefield	SK 131 556	10 miles (16.1km)	1,465ft (445m)	5½ hrs

Comments

An easy-paced walk in tranquil countryside that combines wooded stretches with a ramble along the towpath of the Shropshire Union Canal through a former inland port.

There are grand views and pleasant woodland walking to be enjoyed from the escarpment of Kinver Edge, a popular beauty spot.

A simple but rewarding walk around the lake, where the waterside woods and meadows are full of wildlife and there are impressive views to The Roaches.

A lovely walk from a quiet village across little-visited hills that rise either side of the infant River Hamps. Relax afterwards with something to eat and a drink in the village pub.

'Beating the bounds' rather than delving through the heart of Swynnerton Old Park, this satisfying walk combines panoramic views across rolling Staffordshire with forays through the fringes of this ancient forest.

A lovely rural walk on the edge of Wolverhampton, combining an attractive canal, the wooded course of a disused railway and a thriving local nature reserve.

A canal-side pub waits at the end of this ramble across open countryside, which features waterbirds on a reservoir and a relaxing canal-side stroll.

A restored flint mill and an interesting canal are just two of the highlights of this pleasant walk above the Churnet Valley.

Visit a quiet corner of Staffordshire, where the Dane's wooded gorge cleaves the moorlands and a canal feeder bursts with wildlife.

The Churnet Valley and Dimmings Dale were once centres of industry, but today offer quiet woodland walks with a variety of wildlife to enjoy.

Explore a corner of the vast expanse of Cannock Chase, centred upon the Sherbrook Valley, passing both Commonwealth and German War Graves cemeteries.

Two separate canals and a river are linked on this easy-going ramble through the pleasant south-east corner of Staffordshire's countryside.

An attractive village centred on an interesting parish church, pleasant canal and fine stately home and gardens, all linked in this enjoyable ramble.

An easy ramble with far-reaching views across Shropshire and Staffordshire, linking ancient woodland with a bloody medieval battlefield.

A moorland walk to the tripoint meeting of three of the Peak District's six counties, passing waterfalls and with impressive views to Shutlingsloe, the 'Cheshire Matterhorn'.

The best ridge walk in the whole of Staffordshire, past fantastic weatherworn boulders and with wonderful panoramic views that stretch from Snowdon in Wales to Winter Hill on the Western Pennines.

Voted as one of the Seven Wonders of the Peak, the walk through the narrow gorge of Dovedale reveals one delight after another, while the outward stretch gives fine views to neighbouring Ilam.

Fine views across green uplands of the White Peak and returning via the Manifold Way along the deep, wooded gorge of the River Hamps, although in summer it is often devoid of water.

A beautiful walk in a deeply rural part of mid-Staffordshire, visiting landscaped parkland and tranquil valleys in a little walked, much underrated area.

Literary and music connections ooze from this very pretty corner of Staffordshire where lakes, moorland views, villages and a remarkable mansion await discovery.

There are a couple of attractive canal-side pubs towards the end of this cross-country ramble that links a former railway track and the Shropshire Union Canal.

Rise from the Dove Valley to peaceful Hanbury and the site of England's largest ever explosion before heading for Tutbury's marvellous Norman church and haunting castle.

From an absorbing industrial heritage site, this walk undulates through superb nature reserves before a final flourish along the magnificent wooded gorge of Staffordshire's charming River Churnet.

Plenty of both scenic and historic variety can be enjoyed on this walk that takes you through the finest surviving portions of Cannock Chase.

A magnificent circuit of Staffordshire's stunning Manifold Valley, taking in the memorable Thor's Cave, spectacular wooded gorge and astounding views of the Peak District's White Peak.

A longer but otherwise un-taxing walk from the foot of Holy Austin Rock, incorporating a delightful stretch of the Staffordshire & Worcestershire Canal, returning through a mix of gently rolling woods and open countryside.

The walk begins over Ecton Hill, once the richest copper mine in the world, and takes in an awesome natural cave. The return is along a delightful riverside trail, once the course of a narrow gauge railway.

A lovely walk beside the River Dove through the impressively deep gorge of Wolfscote Dale. For a longer day, head up the dry valley nature reserve of Biggin Dale, where there is a pub in the village.

Keymap

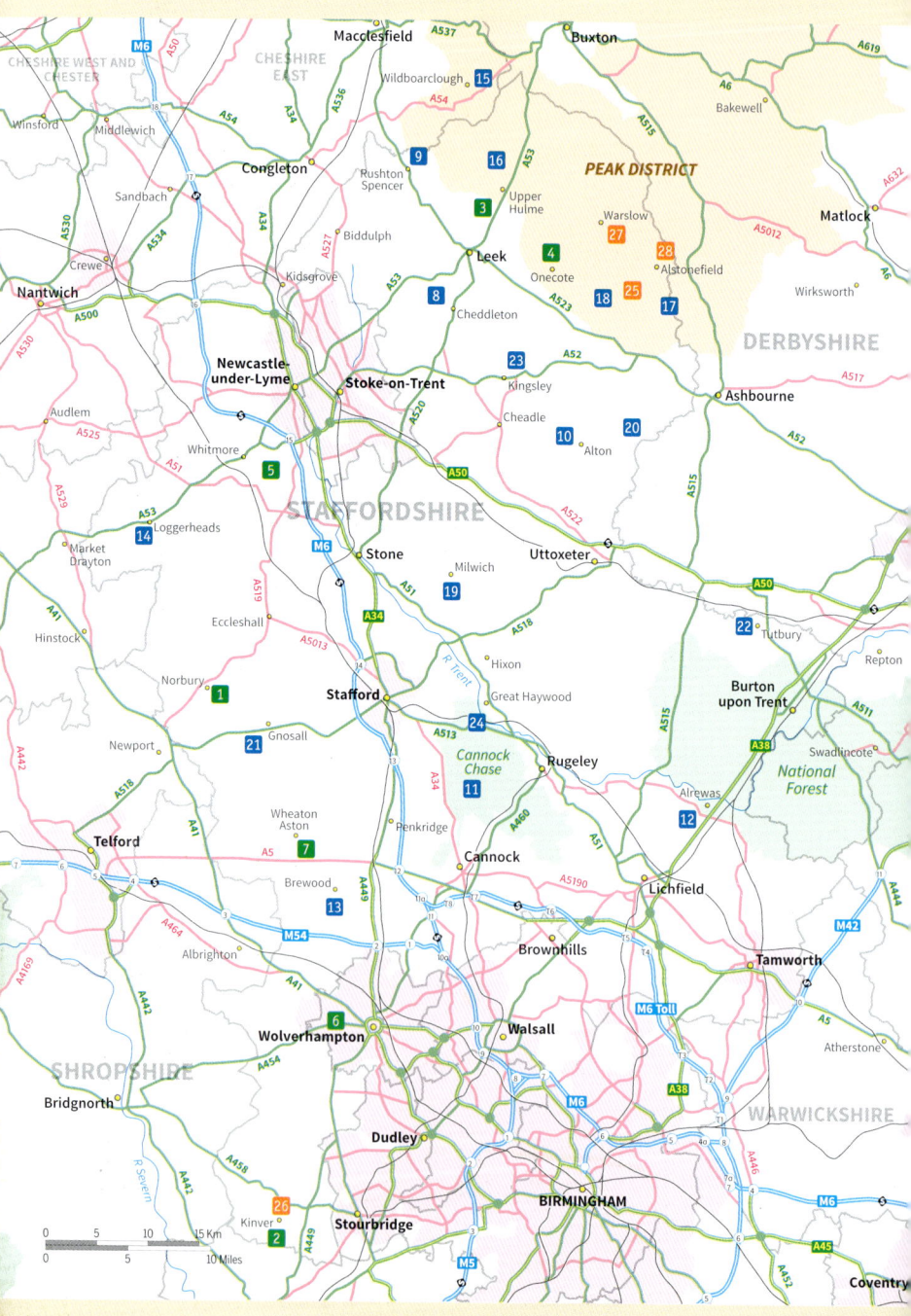

Introduction to Staffordshire

From the southern upsurgence of the Pennine Hills to the fringes of the Midlands' Black Country, Staffordshire offers walkers a tremendous diversity of landscapes to explore. The wild and rugged moorland hills in the north are a stark contrast to the productive agricultural terrain extending across much of the lower-lying ground of the Trent valley, while the vast, unbounded heaths and woods of Cannock Chase are something quite different again. Much of the county is open countryside and woodland, and in many places, the population sparse.

Lie of the land

Staffordshire's northern high ground lies within the Peak District National Park and straddles the boundary between the upturned horseshoe sweep of gritstone and shale that cups a central dome of limestone. Standing out from the rounded, peaty moorland hills, The Roaches and Hen Cloud are splendid examples of rearing escarpments and boulder erosion that are such striking features of the gritstone Dark Peak, while farther east the White Peak is a typical karst (limestone) landscape. The high plateau is deeply incised by narrow, steep-sided gorges such as Dove Dale and the valley of the Manifold, which were created by a massive meltwater run-off at the end of the last ice age. Today's streams and rivers bear no relation to those ancient torrents, and often disappear underground to bubble

Beside the River Dove

Essex Bridge, near Shugborough Hall

up again downstream. The limestone is rich in minerals and deposits of copper were first exploited in the Bonze Age and subsequently, with lead, coal and stone, were worked until the end of the 19th century, very often on a small scale to supplement the income of hill farms. The exception was the copper mine at Ecton, which during the late 18th century was the richest and deepest in the world. Rising beneath the western flanks of the moorland hills, the fast-flowing Churnet powered a range of mills, enabling the establishment of a thriving silk industry at Leek and, lower down, mills at Cheddleton to grind flint, an important ingredient for the pottery industry. It was later discovered that powdered bone served a similar purpose, to produce fine porcelain – bone china. Farther west, the River Dove was renowned for its clarity and a fine trout stream so beloved of Izaak Walton (author of The Compleat Angler) and his friend Charles Cotton. Both rivers are tributaries of the River Trent, the third longest of England's rivers. Its source lies high on Bidulph Moor in Staffordshire's northern corner, and in sweeping south-east and then north-east to leave just beyond Burton upon Trent, drains most of the county. In the 17th century, the Trent too was an excellent fishing river, regarded by Walton as one of the finest in the world, and he suggested that the river was so named because it contained 30 (trente) species of fish, including salmon. In fact, just downstream of Burton, even sturgeons have been caught, weighing up to 250lb (113kg)!

Industry, its rise and decline

During the 18th century, around Burslem and neighbouring villages, the 'Potteries' emerged as one of the pioneers in the Industrial Revolution. The abundance of clay in the area had supported small-scale pottery manufacture since the Middle Ages, but the exploitation of local coal rather than wood to fire the ovens, and the subsequent inventiveness and entrepreneurial skills of people like

Josiah Wedgwood, turned what had been a cottage-based activity into an innovative, mass-production industry that was soon exporting to markets across the world. On the back of Staffordshire's plentiful mineral deposits, similar transformations took place elsewhere, particularly farther south in the Black Country, where abundant coal and ironstone fuelled iron and steel production and gave rise to an assortment of heavy engineering industries. Over to the east, Burton upon Trent became a major centre for the brewing industry, it too exploiting underground resources, in this instance spring water with a chemical hardness that proved excellent for beer making, especially pale ale. At one time there were over 30 separate brewery companies, including Bass, Marston, Worthington, Ind Coop and Burton, which produced a quarter of all the country's beer.

However, none of this burgeoning industry could have evolved without the development of canals. Until then, inland movement of goods depended on cart and packhorse and was consequently slow, expensive and limited in capacity. But almost as soon as England's first 'proper' canal had opened to serve the Duke of Bridgewater's Lancashire coal mines in 1761, Wedgwood recognised its worth and led others in promoting the Trent and Mersey Canal. Other routes quickly followed, connecting the land-locked Midlands to the country's main ports and manufacturing centres. The railways and roads brought ever more capacity and flexibility, enabling Staffordshire to develop as one of the country's most important industrial regions.

The countryside today
The past 70 years or so have seen

Cheddleton Flint Mill

significant change and much of Staffordshire's extractive and heavy industry has now gone, taking with it the pollution that once blighted the county. The canals and many of the railways were abandoned too, but these have found new life in opening endless possibilities for scenic walks to supplement the countless miles of footpaths, tracks, byways and quiet lanes that everywhere criss-cross the landscape. Along these arteries, nature has penetrated the hearts of today's conurbations and pockets of wildlife can be found in the most unlikely settings. Many previously industrial sites have been re-absorbed within their natural setting, often now unrecognisable for what they once were, while others have been preserved for their fascinating industrial heritage. Yet, whatever the conception of Staffordshire might have been, in reality, its industrial past was concentrated in only a few areas.

In many ways, much of Staffordshire remains as it always was; agricultural country and woodland dotted with small villages and farms. Dairy cattle have always been a mainstay of agriculture, with a good deal of the land devoted to grass and fodder crops, though there is some arable farming in the south and east. The open countryside of fields is broken by copses and tracts of woodland, and there are large plantations at Swynnerton, the Maer Hills and Bishop's Wood, while in the east the National Forest project encroaches upon the county. Perhaps the most important area of woodland is the former royal hunting preserve of Cannock Chase. Extending over 26 square miles (67sqkm), it is now designated an Area of Outstanding Natural Beauty and, like the moorlands of the north, has always largely been a wild landscape, its relatively poor soils sparing it from farmland enclosure. Large areas of Access Land and nearly 100 miles (160km) of footpaths, including parts of four separate long-distance trails, offer endless routes for ramblers. Cannock Chase is the largest area of heathland in the Midlands and within its bounds are more than 30 nature, wildlife or conservation sites. It is perhaps one of the best places in the county to spot wildlife, including fallow and red deer as well as smaller mammals, birds, reptiles, and invertebrates.

> This book includes a list of waypoints alongside the description of the walk, so that you can enjoy the full benefits of gps should you wish to. For more information about route navigation, improving your map reading ability, walking with a GPS and for an introduction to basic map and compass techniques, read Pathfinder® Guide *Navigation Skills for Walkers* by outdoor writer Terry Marsh (ISBN 978-0-319-09175-3). This title is available in bookshops and online at os.uk/shop

The Iron Green Man, Tittesworth Water Park

Short walks under 3 hours

walk 1

Norbury Junction and the Shroppie

Start
Canal bridge on A519, ½ mile (800m) north-east of Norbury village

Distance
4¾ miles (7.6km)

Height gain
245 feet (75m)

Approximate time
2¼ hours

Route terrain
Farm tracks, bridlepaths and towpath

Parking
Lay-by at canal bridge on A519

OS maps
Landranger 127 (Stafford & Telford), Explorer 243 (Market Drayton)

GPS waypoints
- SJ 789 242
Ⓐ SJ 794 228
Ⓑ SJ 807 217

Once a busy port at the meeting of two canals, Norbury Junction retains a fascinating atmosphere and remains popular with recreational boaters. This walk skims through pleasant countryside before joining the canal at one of the wonders of the inland waterways.

 Take care in crossing the bridge across the canal; it's very high up and the traffic is considerable. Once over, turn right through the gate, joining the waymarked bridlepath that strings along the edge of pasture and coppice before bending left. It's a well-worn field road; simply remain with it (keep the spinney on your right at an ill-mounted bridleway disc; not through the gate here), presently reaching a T-junction beneath power wires at the corner of a wood.

Turn right along the concreted track, shortly reaching, on your right, the moated site of Norbury Hall. There's an information board providing detail about the site; a country house stood here between the 13th and 19th centuries. It was replaced by the imposing farmhouse immediately to the south; stone from the old manor was used to build the new one. The Anson family, Earls of Lichfield, owned the estate and we'll come across them again shortly. Walk to the minor road at a clutch of houses 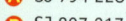.

Turn left and walk to the sharp right bend beyond Brook Cottage; here fork along the field road for Shelmore Fishery. Allow this track to turn right through a gate; you remain on the fieldside path with the mixed woodland on your right, soon entering a wooded track at a corner. One thing you'll probably notice is the large number of pheasants hereabouts; the

---

Shelmore Embankment

Shelmore Embankment, a late work by Thomas Telford, is over a mile (1.6km) long and 60 feet (18m) above the surrounding farmland. It took six years to build, repeated collapses during construction made the entire Birmingham and Liverpool Junction Canal financially unstable. Much of the material used was sourced from the great Grub Street cutting to the north of Norbury. The canal eventually opened in 1835, the last of the great canal projects before the railways came to prominence. The embankment is quite rightly seen as one of the wonders of the canal system.

Norbury estate is still a sporting estate. In the 1830s Lord Anson refused to allow the construction of the new canal across his lands here as it would disturb his shooting; instead the engineer Thomas Telford had to embark on a massive construction project to divert the line to the west. The result is on the far side of the woods; to find it join the surfaced lane ahead right, shortly

Norbury Junction

Norbury Junction marks the place where the Shrewsbury Canal network left the main line. All that's left now are some of the buildings and a short arm used as a boatbuilding and repair yard. It's a fascinating place to wile away a little time. The hire-boat, watering and supply facilities mean it's always busy; here too are a lot of residential moorings. The Shrewsbury Canal was abandoned by 1944; the main line is known as the Shropshire Union Canal (Shroppie) as it was formed in 1846 by the union of a series of individual canals linking Birmingham and Chester.

thereafter reaching a lodge-house and a road **B**.

Turn right and drop down the wooded lane to and beneath an aqueduct. Take care at the far side as you use the steps and gate, left, to climb to the canal towpath, along which turn left.

Beyond **The Junction Inn**, remain on the towpath for another mile (1.6km) to reach an angled path off to the left just before the imposing high bridge over the deep cutting. The lay-by is up this.

NORBURY JUNCTION AND THE SHROPPIE • 11

walk 2

Kinver Edge

Start: Kinver

Distance: 4¼ miles (6.8km); shorter version 2½ miles (4km)

Height gain: 620 feet (190m); shorter version 395 feet (120m)

Approximate time: 2½ hours; shorter version 1½ hours

Route terrain: Paths and quiet back lanes; several short sharp climbs and descents

Parking: Village centre car park

OS maps: Landranger 138 (Kidderminster & Wyre Forest), Explorer 219 (Wolverhampton & Dudley)

GPS waypoints:
- SO 845 834
- Ⓐ SO 838 828
- Ⓑ SO 829 825
- Ⓒ SO 829 822
- Ⓓ SO 831 815
- Ⓔ SO 835 820
- Ⓕ SO 845 829

With its steep wooded hillsides, extensive footpaths and fine views, the prominent sandstone escarpment of Kinver Edge, now protected by the National Trust, Staffordshire and Worcestershire councils, is very popular with walkers. It is also famed for its rock houses, caves excavated from the sandstone. The full walk has two climbs and two steep descents; the shorter version omits Kinver and starts at point Ⓐ, where there are parking facilities.

The former iron forging village of Kinver lies in the valley of the River Stour which also contains the Staffordshire and Worcestershire Canal, built by Brindley to create a link between the River Severn and the Trent and Mersey Canal. High above the village stands the church, built of the local red sandstone.

Start at the car park opposite the parish council building, turn left into the main street and after a few paces swing right by the clock tower and library up Vicarage Drive; soon the lane ends and at a public footpath sign bear right on to an uphill track which curves to the right. At the next public footpath sign, in front of a gate, turn left through a metal gate and walk along a narrow path, between hedges on the right and a fence on the left. The path descends to a lane; turn right along it, avoid the turning to Kinver Scout Training Camp on the left and continue to a T-junction. Turn left and head uphill. At the top of the hill turn right through a barrier by a National Trust sign, opposite the junction with Church Hill Ⓐ. *This is the starting point for the shorter version of the walk.*

Immediately the path forks; take the left turning, keeping ahead down the slope along the right edge of woodland. Pass through a kissing-gate and alongside wire fencing to a second gate. Keep right at the immediate fork. Continue to reach the rim of the escarpment Ⓑ and here a splendid view unfolds, over the steep, thickly wooded slopes of the Edge. Coming in from the right at this point is the Staffordshire Way. Keep left here, through a barrier and beside a NT sign for Kinver Edge. Follow the path along the top of Kinver Edge to the next barrier and enter the Kingsford Forest Park. Beyond the sign, at an oak tree, a waymark points straight on for the Staffordshire Way and North Worcestershire Path Ⓒ.

Turn right here and descend through the trees. Follow the cinder path as it bends sharp left, avoiding a path running off to the right by some wooden posts. Keep to the path and follow it down to Vale's Rock, one of the area's cave dwellings, on the

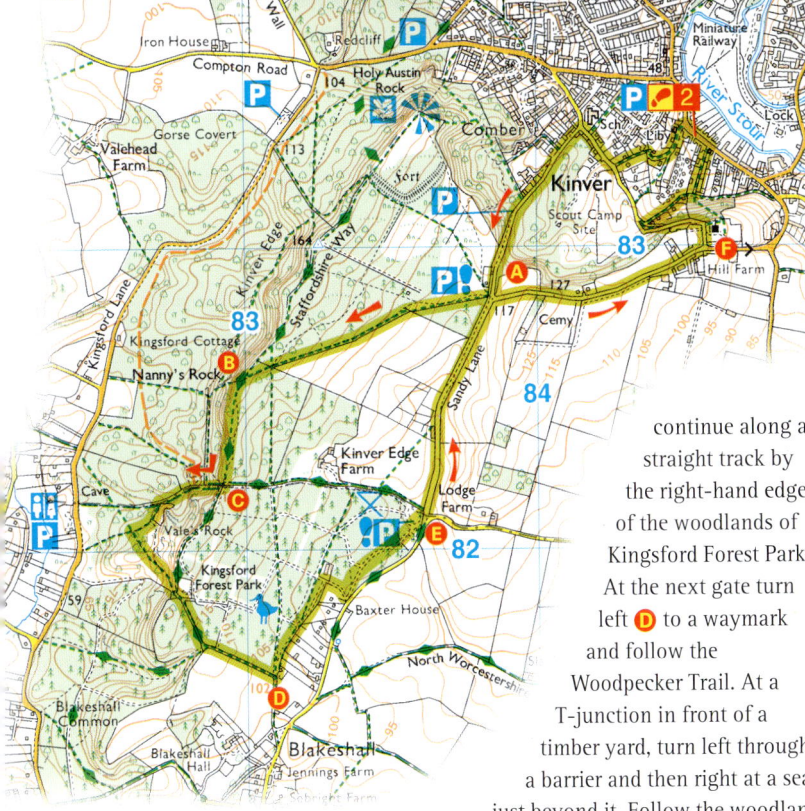

continue along a straight track by the right-hand edge of the woodlands of Kingsford Forest Park. At the next gate turn left **D** to a waymark and follow the Woodpecker Trail. At a T-junction in front of a timber yard, turn left through a barrier and then right at a seat just beyond it. Follow the woodland path to an intersection and follow the route signposted 'car park' – the right-hand path of the two facing you. Maintain the same direction to reach a lane by a car park for Kingsford Forest Park **E**. Turn left at the lane and pass the entrance to Kinver Edge Farm. Keep ahead until you reach Church Hill **A**.

This is the finishing point for those doing the shorter version of the walk.

Turn right, continue as far as Kinver church and turn left **F** along the lane that passes in front of it. The lane bends sharply to the left, heads downhill and then bends sharply to the right. At a footpath sign turn very sharply right along a track which soon bears left and heads downhill in front of houses. Turn left by the wall of a house, head down some steps and continue along a downhill path leading directly back to the centre of Kinver. At the main street turn left and back to the car park where the walk began.

left. Keep left at a path junction just beyond it and walk up to a junction of tracks. Continue to the next junction on the brow of the hill and here turn left to follow a winding uphill path between trees and bracken, climbing steeply to regain the top of the Edge. Pass alongside a fence enclosing a service reservoir on the left and after a few steps you reach a fork. Keep right here.

At a T-junction of tracks, turn left and pass beside another barrier to

Rock houses

A number of rock houses cut into Kinver Edge were permanently inhabited between Georgian times and the early 1960s. Around 12 families made a home here in these real-life hobbit-holes; most were industrial workers in the local iron and broom-making trades.

walk 3

Tittesworth Water

Start: Tittesworth Water Park
Distance: 5 miles (8km)
Height gain: 410 feet (125m)
Approximate time: 2½ hours
Route terrain: Waterside paths
Parking: Car park at start
OS maps: Landranger 118 (Stoke on Trent & Macclesfield), Explorer OL24 (The Peak District, White Peak)
GPS waypoints:
- SJ 993 601
- Ⓐ SJ 991 605
- Ⓑ SJ 991 586
- Ⓒ SJ 995 592
- Ⓓ SJ 996 602

Tucked high beneath the hills that hold the source of the River Churnet, Staffordshire's second largest reservoir, Tittesworth, was built to provide water for the homes and industries of Leek and the Potteries. Today it is also managed as a haven for local wildlife and this walk around its perimeter on the fringe of the Staffordshire Moorlands is an ideal ramble for naturalists.

From the Visitor Centre, head out along the main drive. Reaching the road, go left over a causeway separating the main body of water from the upper section. There is no continuous path around the northern shore, which is set aside as a nature reserve, but hides overlooking the water are signed off on each bank. On the far side of the bridge, look for a path leaving through a gate on the left Ⓐ.

Signed as the Reservoir Trail, it crosses open meadows set back from the water before winding in to cross a couple of streams separated by a small wooded promontory. Carry on at the edge of more meadow before joining a drive to the Watersports Centre. Beyond a jetty, the path resumes, shortly meandering into trees and dipping across another tributary. Farther on, a boardwalk crosses a marshy section into more trees, the path later breaking out along the top edge of Hind's Clough Wood. Eventually reaching a junction, go left. After then bending right, watch for the marked path swinging left again (ignore the grass trail ahead) to drop more steeply down steps to the dam Ⓑ.

Cross the dam and follow a stepped path at the far side into trees. The way soon falls across the foot of Troutsdale before doubling back by the shore, where breaks in the trees give a view to the dam. Later climbing above Springbank Wood, the view is then to the Staffordshire Moors. Reaching a junction Ⓒ, take the left branch, signed as the Crab-apple Trail, which

The Roaches

drops across another stream to continue along the foot of open meadows.

After coming back together again, the path crosses a stream to another fork. As before, keep left and then go left again at the next split, now on a lesser path, which stays nearer the lake shore. Breaking out at the edge of more meadow there are views to Hen Cloud and The Roaches. Entering trees at the far side, converging paths cross the River Churnet **D**.

At the junction beyond, again go left to return to the water's edge, passing a children's play area and then a massive chair and couch carved from redwood. Continue onto the point, where there is a small pavilion from which to enjoy a final view along the reservoir. Finally, head across the grass back to the Visitor Centre.

> **Tittesworth Reservoir** Fed mainly from the eastern branch of the River Churnet, the Tittesworth Reservoir was originally constructed in 1858 to deliver compensation water to the mills downstream. A century later the Staffordshire Potteries Water Board increased its capacity to provide water supplies across North Staffordshire. Work began in 1959 and involved effectively building a new, higher dam just downstream of the original. Because it would now be used for domestic water supply, a purification plant was included in the works. When completed in 1963 the surface area of the lake more than trebled. Since the 1990s the area has been developed as a recreational resource, with footpaths around its shores and the provision of various water activities. The woodlands, meadows and wetlands which surround the lake are valuable habitats for flowers, birds, insects and other wildlife and the northern part of the reservoir is set aside as a nature reserve.

TITTESWORTH WATER • 15

Onecote and the Upper Hamps

Start	Onecote
Distance	5 miles (8km)
Height gain	565 feet (175m)
Approximate time	2½ hours
Route terrain	Field paths, tracks and lane
Parking	Parking by village hall at start (donations)
OS maps	Landranger 119 (Buxton, Matlock, Bakewell & Dovedale), Explorer OL24 (The Peak District, White Peak)
GPS waypoints	SK 049 551 Ⓐ SK 052 555 Ⓑ SK 052 571 Ⓒ SK 053 580 Ⓓ SK 046 581 Ⓔ SK 045 573 Ⓕ SK 046 553

In contrast to the wooded gorge of its lower section and confluence with the Manifold, the upper reaches of the River Hamps lie amongst the expansive rolling foothills of the Peakland Pennines, where scattered farmsteads rather than nucleic villages are the characteristic settlement. Though lacking the ruggedness of the upper moors, this is pleasant walking in relatively 'undiscovered' countryside.

From the Village Hall, walk down to the main lane and go left through the village past **The Jervis Arms**. Cross the River Hamps and walk on for another ¼ mile (400m) before branching off left on a track to Butterton Moor End Farm Ⓐ. Keep ahead through the yard and past the farmhouse to a small gate beside a barn. Over a stile, bear right across a paddock. Cross a farm track and carry on uphill from field to field, later closing with the right wall and then cresting Golden Hill, where a small barn stands over to the left. Crossing a track, continue beside the right boundary, shortly watching for a small bridge spanning the ditch below. Head out across the rough field, crossing an intervening bridge before climbing to a gate at the top. Stay by the left fence, joining a track that leads over a cattle-grid and down to a farm at Black Brook Ⓑ.

Go left through a gateway out of the yard and then swing right, walking past outbuildings and on along a grass swathe beside a stream. Fording it at the top, climb to a small gate. Keep going in the next field and then on through a small grove of hawthorn, the way opening beyond to grazing meadow. Continue uphill, closing with the left boundary and making for a house at Breech that eventually appears on the skyline. Leave over a stile in the top left corner onto a narrow lane Ⓒ.

Go left through a gate, but as the lane then swings left, instead climb the steep bank in front. Carry on straight up the hill, soon meeting the road again at the top. The actual summit of the hill, marked by a trig column, lies along the lane to the right, however, the onward route lies across the stile opposite. Head downhill, ignoring a farm track, to reach a fence stile, just a little way right of two gates. Maintain the same line down the next two fields, then in the fourth, bear half-right to locate a stile in the bottom boundary where the fence meets a hedge. Over that, slant back left down a steep bank to a bridge over a

Upper Acre

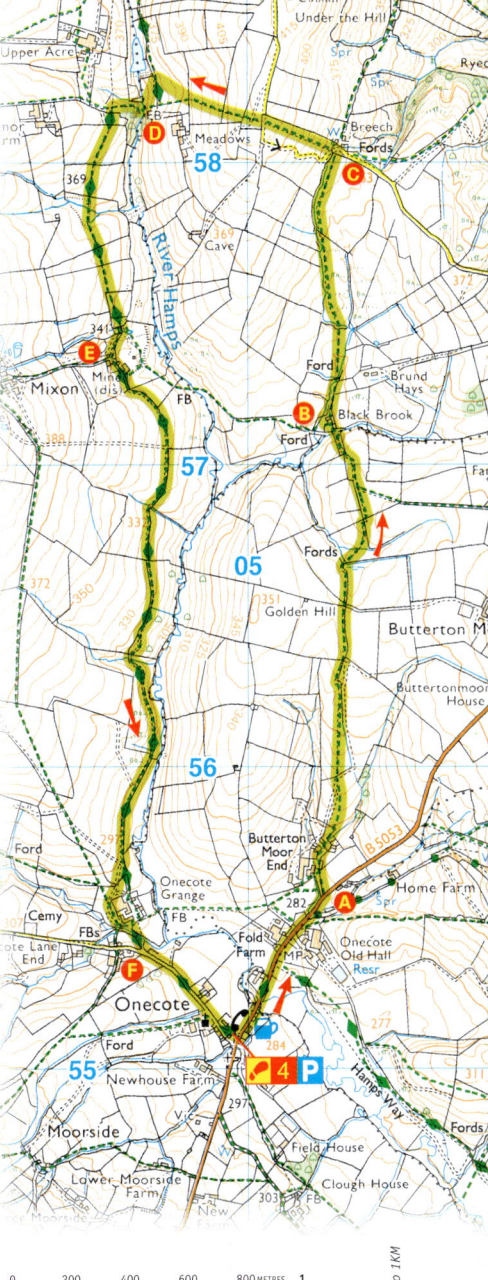

> **Mixon Copper Mine** The workings at Mixon began as a stone quarry towards the end of the 17th century, but then viable amounts of copper, lead and coal were discovered and worked until around 1830. The remains of the small dam on the hillside just to the north held back a small reservoir, which provided a head of water for driving machinery at the mine.

stream – the infant River Hamps **D**.

Climb away through butterbur to a stile and continue up the field beyond to meet the corner of a field track. Follow it left through a gateway and on along a trod across the hillside. In the third field, pass below a short 'causeway' that was, in fact, the dam of a small hillside reservoir. Streams still issue from the breach at its southern end. Walk on across the fields, joining a ditch that leads towards trees concealing the site of the abandoned Mixon Mine. As you approach, a track develops, at the top of which, bear left to a stile near a barn. Cross a small, rough enclosure to emerge on the end of a track by a cottage **E**.

Follow it ahead, passing out through a gateway. The track winds on down the valley for some 1¼ miles (2km) above the infant River Hamps. Eventually, approaching Onecote Grange, keep right at a fork to skirt around the farm. Stay with it across a stream and walk up to meet a lane **F**. Follow it left back to the village.

ONECOTE AND THE UPPER HAMPS • 17

walk 5

Swynnerton Old Park

Start
Hanchurch Hills Picnic Site

Distance
5¾ miles (9.3km)

Height gain
510 feet (155m)

Approximate time
2¾ hours

Route terrain
Woodland and field tracks, a short stretch along a lane

Parking
Car park at start

OS maps
Landranger 118 (Stoke-on-Trent & Macclesfield) and 127 (Stafford & Telford), Explorer 258 Stoke-on-Trent & Newcastle-under-Lyme

GPS waypoints
- SJ 839 397
- Ⓐ SJ 846 391
- Ⓑ SJ 831 391
- Ⓒ SJ 817 394
- Ⓓ SJ 822 409

Numerous paths wander through this ancient park and for anyone confident in reading a map, there are endless trails to explore at will. The described walk however 'beats the bounds' around its edge, and gives a wide perspective of this lovely countryside on the edge of the Potteries towns.

Swynnerton Old Park

Forestry and woodland covers much of Swynnerton Old Park, which has become a popular area for country walks. Pine, spruce and larch dominate the plantation areas but elsewhere you will find beech, oak, silver birch and horse chestnut trees. Managed by Forestry England, the future plan includes the restoration of ancient woodland and expansion of native species, creating diverse habitats for birds, insects and other wildlife, while at the same time continuing sustainable commercial timber production. As a medieval hunting park, the area would have been managed for the benefit of game and there is still plenty of wildlife about. Fallow deer might be spotted if you go quietly, as well as squirrels, foxes and stoats. Listen out too for woodpeckers.

Start from a fork in the track that leads from the lane to the parking areas, taking the left branch - Harley Thorn Lane. Beyond a barrier, it heads past the Hanchurch Reservoir, which is dominated by its 19th-century water tower. Continue down at the edge of the hill, from which there are views across the Trent valley to the Potteries towns.

Through a gate at the end Ⓐ, go right on a track past Harley Thorn House. Where it subsequently swings into the farm, keep ahead on a gently descending trail that runs at the edge of woodland. Approaching another gate, watch for the Hanchurch Walk branching off right. It continues as a woodland path within the fringe of trees. Ignore paths off right, eventually dipping through a clearing and rising to meet a track. Follow it up right to emerge onto a lane Ⓑ.

Cross to the barriered forest track diagonally opposite, but then immediately branch off left onto a path. Where that later forks, keep left on the higher ground to return to the edge of the wood. At the end, go left again, walking a little farther to find a gap out onto a parallel lane. To the right, it ultimately leads out past Shelton under Harley Farm onto another lane **C**.

Follow it right down the hill. Reaching a bend at the bottom, turn off right onto a hedged track. An old by-way, it climbs easily beside a stream for nearly a mile (1.6km) to meet a junction. Go right along a sunken way, dipping across a stream and rising to a fork. Keep right, and climb to a lane **D** and follow it right.

Beyond a couple of houses at its end, the lane degrades to a track and eventually leads to a left-hand bend at Hobgoblin Gate. Ignore the stile and gate on the right and walk round the bend up to a junction with a crossing path. Follow that right, back into the wood. Keep right at a fork and continue climbing onto the more open ground of Hanchurch Heath. Stick with the main track ahead for another ½ mile (800m), finally dropping past a forestry yard to the lane opposite the entrance to Hanchurch Hills picnic site and car park.

Looking across to Trentham Park from Harley Thorn Lane

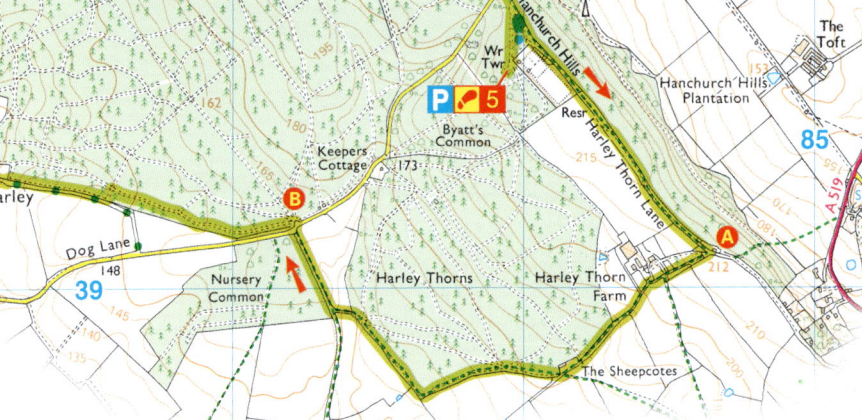

walk 6

The Smestow Valley

Start
Smestow Valley Nature Reserve

Distance
6 miles (9.7km)

Height gain
225 feet (70m)

Approximate time
2¾ hours

Route terrain
Canal towpath, former railway track, field paths

Parking
Car park at start

OS maps
Landranger 139 (Birmingham & Wolverhampton), Explorer 219 (Wolverhampton & Dudley)

GPS waypoints
- SO 891 999
- Ⓐ SO 860 973
- Ⓑ SO 865 967

Only a stone's throw from Wolverhampton's city centre, this walk explores the Smestow Valley, a gem of a rural idyll. After starting out along the Staffordshire & Worcestershire Canal, there is a brief section across open fields before returning along the thickly wooded line of the former Wombourne branch railway line. If you've time to spare, there's plenty more to explore in the woods and meadows of the Smestow Valley Nature Reserve, a fascinating transport heritage museum at the start, and the wonderful Wightwick Manor, noted for its fine pre-Raphaelite art collection.

Wombourne Branch Railway

It was initially developed in 1858 as a goods spur from the main line at Brierley Hill to serve the many collieries, brick and iron works in the area, but a plan was put forward in 1905 to extend the line north to join the main line at Oxley. Construction only began in 1913 and the First World War further delayed completion, and so it was not until 1925 that services began operating. However, the hoped-for passenger numbers never materialised and by 1932 only goods traffic remained. The line was eventually closed in 1968 and the track removed, but re-born six years later as a recreational 'green corridor' path, which runs for over five miles (8km) between Wombourne, near Bratch Locks, and Aldersley, near Oxley Junction.

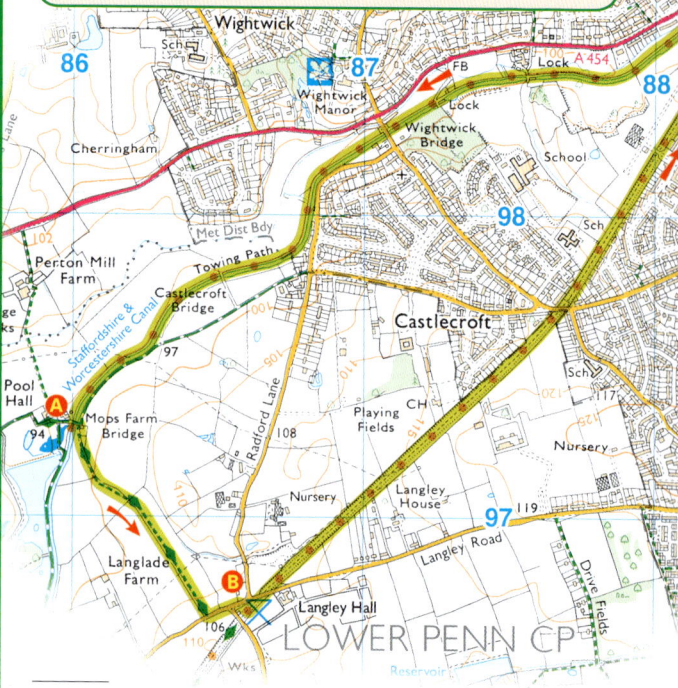

🥾 Walk onto the old station platform by the **Cupcake Lane** café, where steps drop to the railway trackbed. Cross to the path opposite and at its end, go left to emerge onto a track. Turn right over Smestow Brook and then, just before the canal bridge, right again down to the towpath.

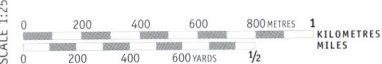

Head away, shortly passing beneath a girder bridge that carried the former railway. A little farther on is Compton Lock, beside which is one of canal engineer Brindley's 'lobsterpot' weirs. A feature of this canal, they drain excess water around the lock, the distinctive domed iron grill preventing debris from blocking the drain. Just beyond, the canal passes beneath Compton Road Bridge.

The canal and railway have so far kept company, but the canal now wanders away, dropping through another couple of locks before passing beneath Wightwick Bridge. The National Trust's Wightwick Manor is close by and this is the point at which to leave the canal if you wish to visit. Otherwise, carry on with the towpath for another mile (1.6km) to Mops Farm Bridge (No. 54) 🅐.

Climb onto the track above and cross the bridge. Where it then immediately bends in front of a house, turn off right along a field-edge path. Later on, slip beside a redundant stile to continue with the hedge now on your right, eventually emerging onto a lane. Walk left, passing a road junction, just beyond which is a lay-by on your right 🅑. Cross the picnic area behind and go down steps to the old trackbed, running within a deep, wooded cutting. Follow it away to the left. The line runs arrow straight for nearly a mile (1.6km) before passing beneath a road bridge at Castlecroft. If looking for refreshment, a path climbs back on the right immediately after the bridge to the road above. You will then find the **Firs Inn** a short distance to the right.

The way back continues along the former railway, which is now bordered on the left by the Smestow Valley Nature Reserve. Paths loop off through wood and meadow areas, which stretch across to the canal. A little farther on, an overgrown platform is all that remains of Compton Halt, which only operated for seven years before its closure in 1932. Just beyond, the railway crosses the road at Compton and continues to the girder bridge passed on the outward leg. The way then weaves right and left to a footbridge over Smestow Brook, necessary as the original railway bridge has been 'lowered', a polite euphemism for 'demolished'. Over the bridge bear right and continue with the railway back to Tettenhall Station, from which you began. ●

walk 7 Wheaton Aston

Start
Wheaton Aston

Distance
6 miles (9.7km)

Height gain
235 feet (70m)

Approximate time
2¾ hours

Route terrain
Tracks, towpaths and lane

Parking
Car park off Hawthorne Road in village

OS maps
Landrangers 127 (Stafford & Telford), Explorer 242 (Telford, Ironbridge & The Wrekin)

GPS waypoints
- SJ 852 126
- Ⓐ SJ 853 111
- Ⓑ SJ 854 107
- Ⓒ SJ 855 100
- Ⓓ SJ 863 095
- Ⓔ SJ 875 099
- Ⓕ SJ 855 129

One of the big problems faced by 18th- and 19th-century canal surveyors was the provision of reliable and copious water supplies. As a consequence, many reservoirs were constructed such as that at Belvide, built to feed the Shropshire Union Canal. Now a noted nature reserve (permits required to visit the reserve itself), it is passed on this relaxing countryside walk from the attractive village of Wheaton Aston, which concludes with a pleasant stretch beside the canal.

 Out of the village car park, turn left along Hawthorne Road. Swing right at the bottom and then go left in front of St Mary's Church along Mill Lane. At the end, where it bends right, leave over a stile on the left into the corner of a field. Head away by a fence on the right. Come out at the far side onto a contained track and follow it away to the right.

Later losing the right hedge, carry on at the edge of successive fields. Eventually reaching a redundant stile, walk forward across a small field to a footbridge. Over that, wind right and left within the field corner and walk on to find a stile part-way along the right-hand fence. Head diagonally left across a paddock to another stile behind a house and continue past topiary to leave over a third stile into a field. Head out on the same line, aiming just left of a solitary tree to meet a track by a redundant stile Ⓐ. Cross and strike out towards the far

Looking back to Wheaton Aston

hedge. Follow it right, towards a farm. Reaching the field corner, go over a stile by a gate on the left. Turn right beside the boundary past a pond to leave at the corner into a farmyard. If the stile there is impassable because of mud, remain

The Belvide Reservoir

The lock at Wheaton Aston takes the canal onto its summit stretch, which runs for 8 miles (13km) to its southern junction at Autherley. The main water supply is the Belvide Reservoir, but even as the canal opened, it was apparent that it was insufficient to meet the level of traffic using the canal. A decision was taken to double its capacity and the work completed in 1842. The large body of water attracts numerous species of birds and has been designated an SSSI, managed by the West Midland Bird Club. There are stretches along the footpath from which the water can be seen, although a permit is required to enter the nature reserve and its hides.

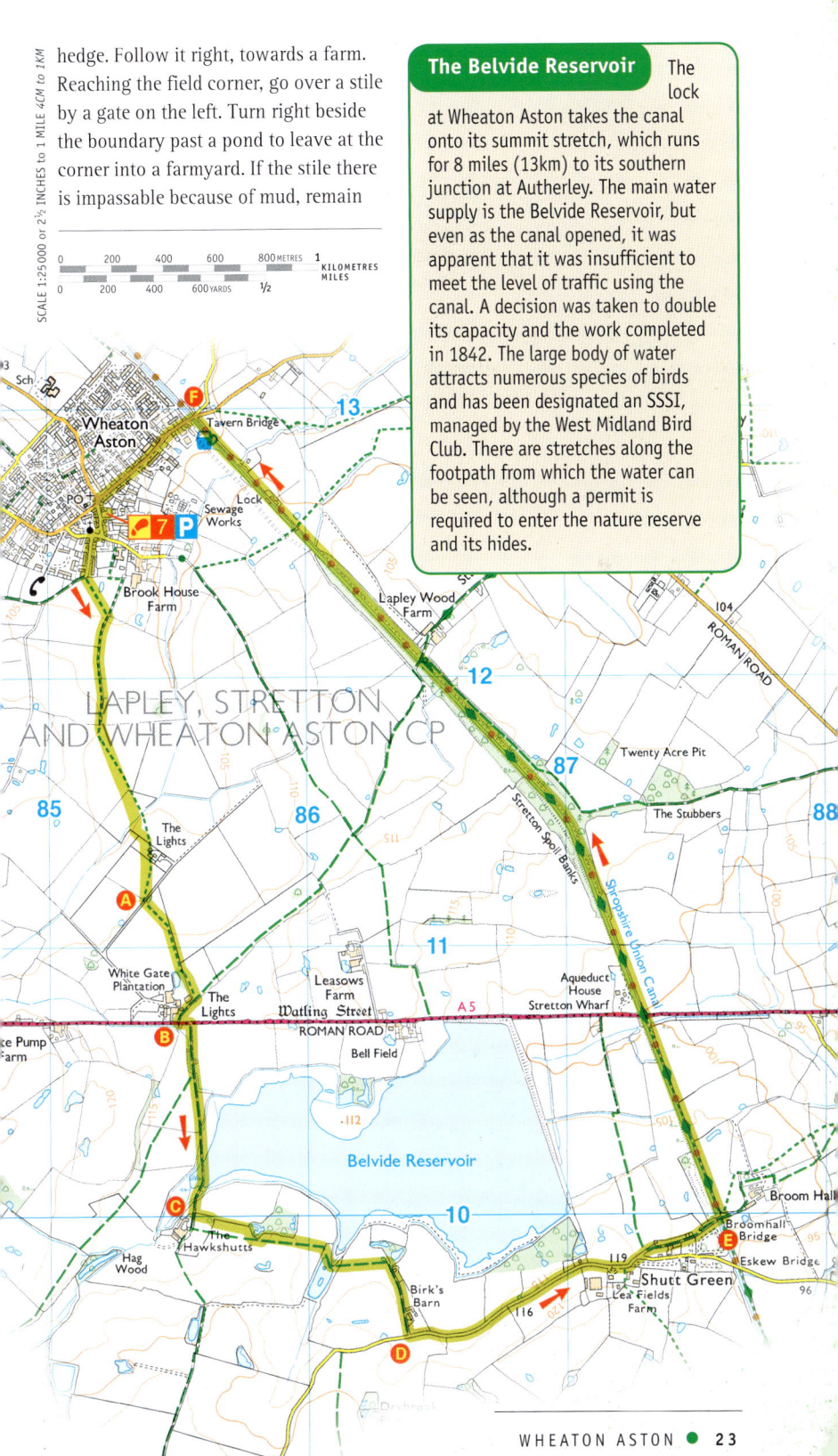

WHEATON ASTON ● 23

Watling Street Aqueduct

within the field, following the fence around left and right to a bridle gate. Walk out along the bottom of the yard past stock sheds and along a short grass track to the main road **B**.

Briefly follow the verge left and cross to a drive to Hawkshutt Farm and Anvil Cottage. It leads past the western shore of the Belvide Reservoir, which is initially hidden behind a hedge. Beyond a bridge, carry on past a gate into the nature reserve (accessible by permit only) to a second gate on the left, just a little farther along **C**. Head away by the left fence, continuing in a second field along a track towards a small wood. Skirt around its edge and keep going to another gate at the far side of the field. Wind on through a copse and cross another field beyond to emerge onto the end of a track behind a cottage. Follow it away to the right, passing Birk's Barn and eventually coming out onto a lane **D**.

Follow the lane left for a little over ½ mile (800m) towards Shutt Green. After passing Lea Fields Farm, branch off left along a contained path signed beside a drive to a cottage. It leads past the buildings and small holding to a bridge over the Shropshire Union Canal **E**. Immediately over the bridge, cross a stile on the right down to the towpath. Double back beneath the bridge and follow the canal north.

Not far along, the canal narrows to cross the A5, Watling Street, on a cast-iron aqueduct supported on stone buttresses. Immediately beyond is Stretton Wharf, one of many spots along the canal where boat repairs were (and still are) carried out. Farther along, the canal enters a wooded cutting known as Stretton Spoil Banks. Emerging beyond, the canal shortly drops through a lock at the edge of Wheaton Aston. Approaching the next bridge (No. 19) **F**, climb to the road above and follow it over the bridge past **The Hartley Arms** into the town. After ¼ mile (400m), at a staggered crossroads, turn left back to the car park.

The Shropshire Union Canal

This stretch of the canal between Nantwich and Wolverhampton was built as the Birmingham & Liverpool Junction Canal to link the Birmingham system with the Ellesmere & Chester Canal and thence to the Mersey. Engineered by Thomas Telford and opened in 1835, it was the last major narrow canal of the trunk network to be built, just as competition from the railways began to gather momentum. Indeed, the formation of the Shropshire Union Railways and Canal Company in 1846 was intended to facilitate conversion of much of the system to rail, but which in the event, did not happen. The canal continued to be an important and profitable route into the 20th century, handling commercial traffic after most of the remaining system had been abandoned at the end of the Second World War and into the mid-1960s.

Near Bromstead Common

Slightly harder walks of 3–4 hours

walk 8

Cheddleton and the Caldon Canal

Start
Deep Hayes Country Park

Distance
5¾ miles (9.3km)

Height gain
645 feet (195m)

Approximate time
3 hours

Route terrain
Towpath, field paths and lane

Parking
Car park at start

OS maps
Landranger 118 (Stoke on Trent & Macclesfield), Explorer OL24 (The Peak District, White Peak) or Explorer 258 (Stoke-on-Trent & Newcastle-under-Lyme)

GPS waypoints
- SJ 960 533
- Ⓐ SJ 956 532
- Ⓑ SJ 944 538
- Ⓒ SJ 939 532
- Ⓓ SJ 947 526
- Ⓔ SJ 958 523
- Ⓕ SJ 968 522
- Ⓖ SJ 972 525

The Caldon Canal is widely heralded one of the most attractive of Britain's industrial waterways and this stretch near Cheddleton certainly lives up to that reputation. Deep Hayes Country Park, from where the walk begins, attracts plentiful waterfowl and other wildlife, while the Flint Mill museum, passed on the return leg, gives a unique insight to some of the area's fascinating industrial heritage.

Head from the car park back down to the lane and immediately turn sharp left onto a barriered track. Walk by the Caldon Canal through trees at the edge of the country park, shortly crossing a stream that emanates from the pools of the former reservoir, by a curious 'sentry box' water gauge. Remain above the canal, soon quitting the woods over a stile into a field. Leaving the canal, follow a wall across a sloping meadow to a farm. Pass through the yard and out along its track to a lane Ⓐ.

Turn right, back down to the canal. Over the bridge, drop right to the towpath and double back under the bridge behind **The Holly Bush Inn**. Around a bend the way passes Hazelhurst Aqueduct, which carries the Leek Branch of the Caldon Canal. Continue past moorings and then a small flight of three locks. Walk under a delicate cast-iron footbridge, just beyond which the two branches of the Caldon Canal come together.

Carry on beside the canal. Leave at the next bridge (No. 34) Ⓑ and cross the canal, the track then winding right to a stile and gate. Head out on a diagonal across a couple of fields. Entering a third field, climb by the left hedge towards Hayes Farm. Over a stile in the top corner of the field, continue beside the right hedge past the farm and out at the top onto a lane Ⓒ.

Go left up the hill. At the top of the brow, branch off left in front of a cottage on a drive to High View and Hollinhurst farms. Where it immediately bends, mount a stile on the right and walk away with the right boundary. Over a stile by a cattle trough, carry on to cross another in the next corner. Turn right, continuing at the edge of successive fields and eventually emerging onto a junction of lanes at Cats Edge Ⓓ.

Take the one opposite. However, after 250 yards, leave over a stile by a gate on the left. Follow a track away, and on at the perimeter of the next field. At the bottom, a track through a gate on the left falls to a junction in front of buildings at Ladygreen. Go right, but where the track then swings left, keep ahead on an old grass track leading into a rough meadow. Walk on at the edge, crossing a plank bridge before bearing away to follow waymarks up a bank. Over a stiled bridge at the top, cross another meadow to come out by Lee House. Follow the track right, over a cattle-grid, and then go left at the junction immediately beyond, the way marked to Cheddleton. Approaching a gate, turn off over a stile on the right and follow the field edge away. Drop over another stile and continue down beside woodland to a junction **E**.

The path to the left offers a shortcut back through Deep Hayes Country Park. However, the route continues ahead, descending more steps to a bridge over a stream. Climb beyond to a waymark and continue ahead with the public footpath towards Cheddleton. At the top of the bank, go right and then left over a stile. Head out across scrubby pasture, rising to a gate at the edge of a field. Strike across to the far right corner and follow a winding track to a small paddock by Shaffalong Farm. Walk on at its left edge to a stile, after which bear right. Cross a grass track and continue the line to another stile in the corner. Keep by the left hedge and pass into a large field. Bearing right, make for a stile in the far wall and head on straight downfield. Cross a track to Hanfield, and carry on across a final field to emerge onto a lane by the former village school, **Old School Tea Rooms F**. Go down through the village to the main road and turn downhill. Just before the bottom, take a track off left signed to the Flint Mill **G**.

Walk down to join the canal towpath, which has emerged from beneath a bridge and building straddling the canal. Follow the towpath away from the bridge for about a mile (1.6km) as far as bridge number 39. Leave the canal there, cross the bridge and turn off right back into Deep Hayes Country Park.

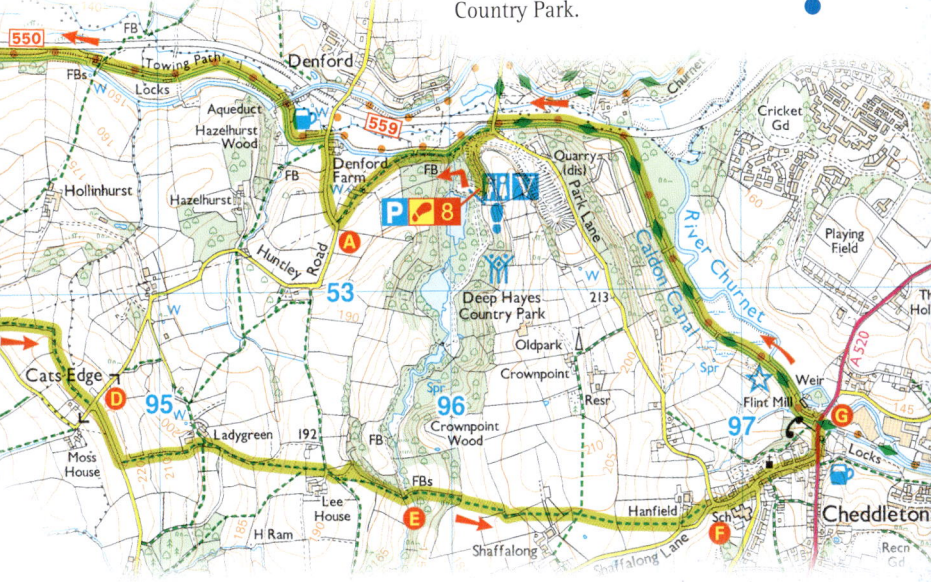

walk 9

Rushton Spencer and the Dane Valley

Start
Rushton Spencer

Distance
5¾ miles (9.3km)

Height gain
660 feet (200m)

Approximate time
3 hours

Route terrain
Undulating, with a few steady climbs. Mix of field paths, lanes and towpath. The towpath may be very muddy in sections

Parking
Public car park off Station Lane beside The Knot Inn (not the pub car park)

OS maps
Landranger 118 (Stoke-on-Trent & Macclesfield), Explorer OL24 (Peak District – White Peak)

GPS waypoints
- SJ 936 624
- Ⓐ SJ 950 626
- Ⓑ SJ 955 642

The River Dane spills from the enfolding moors through a deep wooded gorge at the edge of the Peak District National Park. This walk culminates in a passage through this, reaching it via a remote church and tranquil lanes amid tumbling hills, with some startling views en route.

Return to the **Knot Inn** and turn left past the imposing North Staffordshire Railway station house; then fork left for Rushton Hall. A series of steep bends brings you to the lane to the church; turn left along this. St Lawrence's Church was known as the 'Church in the Wilderness' and is over 600 years old. Its isolated location recalls its function serving a wide rural community hereabouts. Visible beyond pastures to the right, Rudyard Lake snakes towards the horizon.

Leave the churchyard by the hand-gate at the far-left corner, dropping to cross the old railway on an over-bridge, continuing across two pastures to the main road opposite the **Royal Oak** pub. *Cross carefully* and turn right; then go sharp-left past the pub along Sugar Street. Opposite the village school here in Rushton Spencer, turn right up Alley Lane. Wind with this to a sharp-right hairpin bend; here leave the lane and use the stile into pasture. In a few paces fork left on a path through thick holly trees, joining a fieldside path beyond a hand-gate. As the fence turns right at the end of the trees, head half-right to join the lane just right of the house. Go left, dropping into a side valley and a junction. Turn right and walk up to Heaton hamlet.

Keep left at the postbox Ⓐ; then left again along the 'No Through Road'. The views get ever better as this slides along the side of a wide ridge, opening out to encompass Wincle Minn, the higher slopes of Back Forest and the stub-end of The Roaches. Remain on the main track to reach the old hall and barn at Heatonlow. Turn right at the duckpond, crossing the gravelled yard in front of the hall. Use the wall stile and turn left beside the pylon, drifting very gradually away from the

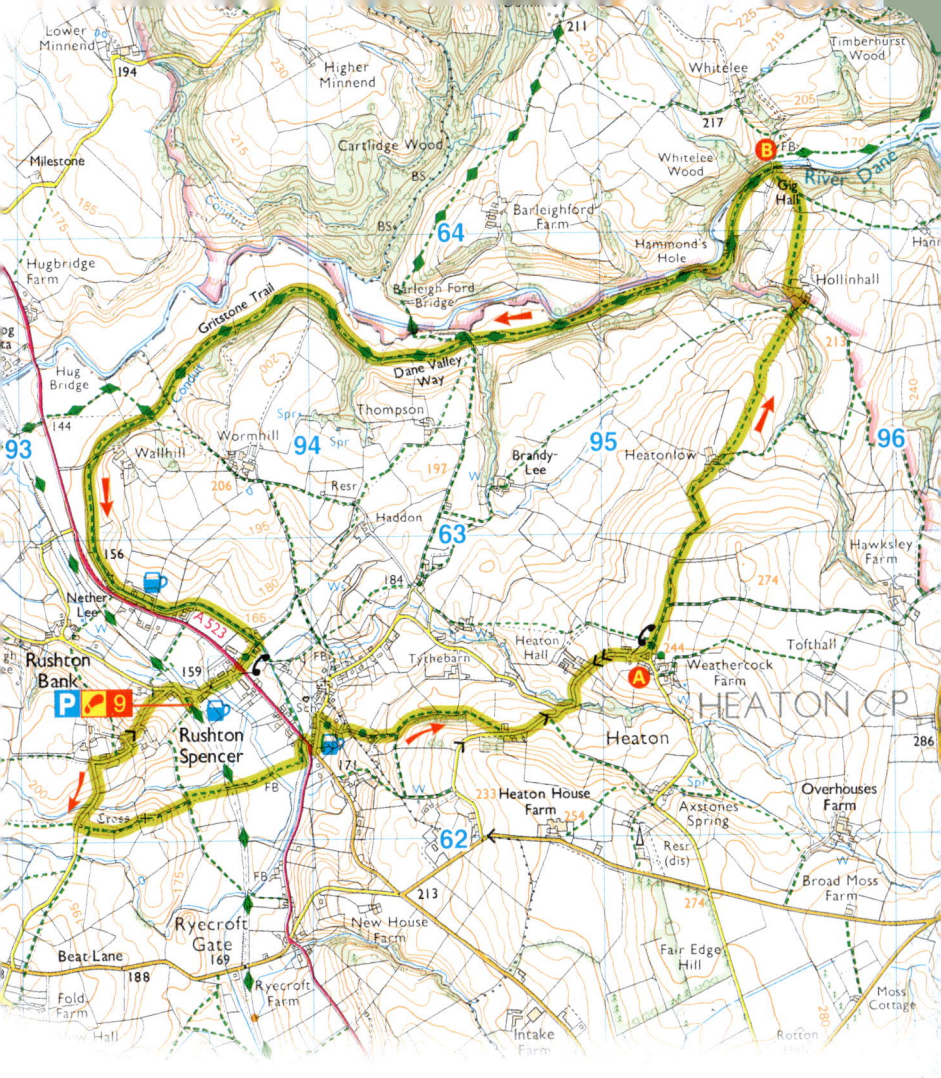

fence-line on your left. The excellent views remain before the way reaches a stile beyond a line of trees and in-line with the stone farmhouse. The path drops steeply into a deep clough, where a footbridge at the foot of steps is a great place to pause in this compact wooded gorge, smothered in ferns, mosses and seasonal flowers.

Tackle the steps beyond and turn left at the fingerpost for Danebridge. Pass beside the barn, through a hand-gate and diagonally across a rough driveway. Look for another stile at the far end of the large barn, take this and keep straight ahead in-line across the sloping pasture (not the field-foot track) to another waymarked stile at the far side. The route crosses reedy pasture, bends left and drops down a set of rough steps beside a television aerial to reach a stile beside the remote house at Gig Hall. Bear right to the footbridge across the River Dane (do not cross it), secluded in this magnificent wooded chasm below Whitelee weir **B**.

Turn left for Barleighford Bridge, putting the leat on your left. Pass by a lengthsman's cottage and remain beside

RUSHTON SPENCER AND THE DANE VALLEY

> **Whitelee Mill** A brace of thundering weirs and a few remains mark the site of Whitelee Mill, a paper mill and possibly earlier a fulling mill treating wool. It's highly likely that an apprentice millwright here in the 1730s was James Brindley, who went on to become a famous canal engineer. The upper weir fed the mill; the weir near the footbridge diverted water into a feeder leat for Rudyard Lake. The mill was demolished in the mid 19th century.

the old watercourse. It was built in 1808 to top up Rudyard Lake, which was created in the late 1790s to supply the distant Trent and Mersey Canal (engineered by Brindley) in Stoke-on-Trent.

It's a lovely, peaceful walk through a wildlife-rich corridor. Stay with the waterside path across a surfaced farm road and through a series of stiles and gates. In a further 1¼ miles (2km) the reedy leat reaches the fringe of Rushton Spencer within trees above the A523, passing behind the old Rushton Inn. Stay with the leat for another 600 yards until you reach a sloping, part-flagged driveway. Turn right down to the main road and cross into Station Lane (opposite) to return to the Knot Inn.

The Dane Valley, near Whitelee Mill

Dimmings Dale and the Churnet Valley

walk 10

Start
The Ramblers' Retreat, Dimmings Dale

Distance
5¾ miles (9.3km)

Height gain
745 feet (225m)

Approximate time
3 hours

Route terrain
Woodland and field paths, former railway track and some lane

Parking
Car park at start

OS maps
Landranger 128 (Derby & Burton upon Trent), Explorer 259 (Derby)

GPS waypoints
- SK 062 431
- Ⓐ SK 052 437
- Ⓑ SK 043 438
- Ⓒ SK 052 431
- Ⓓ SK 050 427
- Ⓔ SK 067 417
- Ⓕ SK 071 426

Before the 18th-century Industrial Revolution, Dimmings Dale and its environs were a hive of industrial activity, exploiting underground ores, the gushing streams and the hillside forests to fuel smelters. But the subsequent Steam Age rendered its way of life obsolete and the Earl of Shrewsbury, whose land it was, transformed the area into a country estate, building Alton Towers and laying out rides through the woodlands. The quiet wooded valleys, streams and pools now attract a wide variety of birds and other wildlife while the rolling countryside offers delightful rambling routes.

Leave the car park and go left past the **Ramblers' Retreat** tearoom, immediately turning left again on a track signed to the Smelting Mill and Earl's Rock. Beyond the mill, now a private residence, the main track runs above the extensive mill pond, which all but fills the base of the valley. After Earl's Rock, also a private residence, the track narrows through a barrier and climbs on up the base of the wooded valley. Ignore side paths until, ultimately emerging from trees at the top, you meet a crossing track Ⓐ. Follow it to the right over a cattle-grid. The drive undulates between pastures for over ½ mile (800m) before eventually falling to a lane Ⓑ.

Turn left down the hill, passing Furnace Farm to a junction by a cottage, Old Furnace. There, turn off beside it, on a track signed back to Dimmingsdale. It soon enters woodland, dropping beside a stream, which lower down flows into a small pool that debouches at its far end over a waterfall. Keep with the descending path, in time reaching a fork where you should take the lower branch past a barrier. The stream shortly broadens into the first of a succession of pools. Carry on to a junction at the foot of the third pool Ⓒ.

There, turn off right across the dam. On the far side curve left on a crossing track but then immediately swing off right on a rising stony path. After a steady pull, the gradient eases to meet a joining path. Go sharp left, shortly winding to a stile at the edge of the wood. Walk down by the left wall through a dip and up to a gap stile in the top wall. Climb across a final meadow to the road at the far side.

Go right but almost immediately cross to a track off left Ⓓ. Approaching a farmhouse, look for a gate into the adjacent

Dimmings Dale

Tucked away in seclusion, the narrow valley of Dimmings Dale is today remarkable for its beauty and a haven for wildlife. Streams, pools, woodland and meadows attract all manner of wildlife; foxes, stoats, hedgehogs and muntjac deer creep through the cover. Birds to be seen include both little and tawny owls, pied flycatchers and redstarts, while on the water are moorhens, herons, Canada geese and kingfishers. But things weren't always so. In the 15th and 16th centuries, the woods were managed for charcoal production used to smelt and work lead and iron. The fast flowing streams were dammed to drive water mills that powered the furnace bellows and forging hammers. The change came in the 19th century when the 15th Earl of Shrewsbury, who owned the Alton estate, appreciated its inherent beauty and set about creating drives, fishing lakes and walks to complement the formal gardens around his new gothic house just across the Churnet Valley.

---

junction. Keep ahead over a rise, but where the street then bends right, leave ahead along a footpath between houses. Dropping to a lower road, go left down the hill and over a causeway bridge spanning the Churnet Valley.

At the far side, turn off left beside a small building **F** and drop to the trackbed of the old Churnet Valley Line. Head away past Alton Station, now a Landmark Trust holiday let. After a little over ½ mile (800m), the trail passes beneath Lord's Bridge. Immediately beyond, climb up right to the track

Alton Station

field on the left and go right beside the fence. Beyond the buildings, ignore a stile out on the right and keep ahead through a gate near the corner. Continue across the next field, keeping left of a small enclosure to a stile in the top fence.

Cross a grass track to another stile and bear left towards the distant corner. Carry on at the edge of a couple more fields. Ignoring a private track, cross a stile and continue at the edge of two more fields. In the final field, bear left to reach a road **E**. Head right downhill to Gallows Green.

Reaching a junction at the edge of the village, a sign indicates a path off left up steps to a stile. Head down at the field edge and then through a scrubby fold. Cross a final small field to emerge beside a house onto another road. Follow it right, rounding a bend to a

Looking across to Dimmingsdale Wood

above. Cross the bridge and then a second one over the River Churnet to come out opposite the Ramblers Retreat. The car park is then just to the left.

walk 11

Cannock Chase and the War Graves

Start
Commonwealth War Cemetery

Distance
6¼ miles (10.1km)

Height gain
520 feet (160m)

Approximate time
3 hours

Route terrain
Heathland paths and tracks

Parking
Car park at start

OS maps
Landranger 127 (Stafford & Telford) and 128 (Derby & Burton upon Trent), Explorer (244 Cannock Chase & Chasewater)

GPS waypoints
- SJ 983 154
- Ⓐ SJ 980 165
- Ⓑ SJ 983 170
- Ⓒ SJ 980 181
- Ⓓ SJ 986 186
- Ⓔ SJ 999 185
- Ⓕ SJ 998 168
- Ⓖ SJ 989 165

Large areas of Cannock Chase were commandeered for military use during two Worlds Wars, with training camps, a hospital and prisoner of war camps being built across the heath. It is perhaps fitting that this now peaceful and lovely location was chosen for the site of Commonwealth and German war cemeteries, as well as a memorial to the Polish victims of the Katyn Massacre.

From the parking area by the Commonwealth War Cemetery, follow the drive towards the German War Cemetery. However, just through the barrier, turn off left on a path at the edge of the heath behind the Commonwealth cemetery. At the corner of the cemetery, turn right. Ignore a subsequent crossing, the path beyond then gently bending left and in time turning parallel to a gravel track. Move to the right and follow it on to a small car park. Continue ahead with the ongoing gravel track. At a junction a short way along, go right and then immediately left. Stick with this path, eventually entering trees and dipping to another crossing. To the left is the road and a tea room at **Springslade Lodge**. The ongoing walk, however, is

Wartime camps

With the outbreak of war in 1914, there was an immediate call for volunteers, which raised thousands of men to be processed and trained. Amongst others up and down the country, two camps were established on Cannock Chase, Rugeley (by Rifle Range Corner) and Brocton (just south of the present village), which between them could accommodate 40,000 soldiers, and it is estimated that over half a million troops passed through during the war. Initially transit camps, they quickly developed as full training facilities and were serviced by a railway – the Tackeroo Express. Cannock became the headquarters for the 5th Battalion New Zealand Rifle Brigade, whose experiences on the Somme and Messines were put to use in training new recruits. At Brocton there were also two POW camps, with those fit enough to work being employed within the camps and surrounding area. To serve them all, a 1,000-bed hospital was built at Brindley Heath, which was also used to treat wounded soldiers returning from the front. After the war, all the camps were dismantled, although foundations remain amongst the trees and there is an army cadet training centre on the site of Rugeley Camp.

to the right, climbing a short distance to the Katyn Memorial, which stands back from the path on the left **A**.

Turn off to the memorial to find a narrower path passing beside it on the right into the trees. Keep ahead as another joins from the right and walk on to meet a wider path. Go left a few yards to a broad crossing path and follow that right. Carry on, ignoring paths off on the right until you reach an obvious junction, where the main track swings left **B**. Take that (if you pass a crumbling marker stone you have gone a little too far).

Shortly reaching a diagonal crossing, fork right and then shortly after, keep ahead over a six-way junction. Stick with the main track for another ½ mile (800m), eventually reaching a junction at the crest of the rise where you will see a trig column over to the left. Go to that, and then turn right to find the Glacial Boulder a few yards away **C**.

Turn right again, back to the main

CANNOCK CHASE AND THE WAR GRAVES • 35

path and follow it left for 75 yards. There, turn off right onto a broad path that undulates across the open heath. Ignoring junctions, keep with the path ahead, which shortly settles along a rounded spur before descending to meet a crossing path along the base of the Sherbrook Valley **D**.

Take the path opposite over a footbridge and climb away up the other side of the valley. Joining a track from the left, continue steadily up a wooded fold to reach a double crossing at the top. Keep ahead into trees, ignoring another crossing to continue on a broader path. Go forward again at the next junction, where you will notice the high embankment of a former firing range over to the left. At the far end of the bank, cross a forest road and stick with the ongoing track, which now loses height into another valley, that of Old Brook **E**.

At the bottom, turn right, rising above the stream to a junction with a broad forest road. Go left, but after 75 yards look for a narrow path leaving on the right. It leads through trees to another broad track. Follow that right past a concrete embankment (part of another firing range). At the end of the bank, go right again and then keep ahead with the main track as it immediately forks. Follow that on for over ¾ mile (1.2km), after a while passing the buildings of an army cadet training camp and ultimately emerging past a barrier and car park to meet a road at Rifle Range Corner **F**.

However, just before the road, turn off right past a barrier onto another track. Gently descending, it bends left past a junction. Ignore another later junction and continue down eventually reaching a crossing at the base of the valley **G**. Now go left, climbing beside a fence to a fork. Bear left beside the fence, shortly passing a waypost at Gospel Place. Remain with the main track as it bends to the right and keep going past another crossing. The way then becomes metalled past the German War Cemetery. Carry on along the drive, which leads back to the parking area. ●

The Commonwealth War Cemetery

Fradley Junction

Fradley Junction, where the Coventry Canal meets the Trent & Mersey, was reputedly one of the busiest in the country, while just to the north-east, the canal system intersects the River Trent. This gentle walk explores sections of both canals between two attractive villages and includes a local waterside nature reserve as well.

walk 12

Start
Fradley Junction

Distance
6½ miles (10.5km)

Height gain
140 feet (45m)

Approximate time
3 hours

Route terrain
Canal towpath, field paths and some lane

Parking
Car park at Fradley Junction (Pay & Display)

OS maps
Landranger 128 (Derby & Burton upon Trent), Explorer (245 The National Forest)

GPS waypoints
- SK 142 141
- Ⓐ SK 173 156
- Ⓑ SK 163 149
- Ⓒ SK 162 138
- Ⓓ SK 157 133

The Trent & Mersey and Fradley Junction

Part of Brindley's grand scheme to link the main industrial areas of the country, the Trent & Mersey Canal runs for over 93 miles (150km) between the River Trent at Derwent Mouth and the Bridgewater Canal, by which it enters the River Mersey. Incorporating 76 locks, over 200 bridges and the Harecastle Tunnel (over 1½ miles/2.4km long), all dug and built by hand, it took only 11 years to complete and was fully open by 1777. One of the main proponents of the scheme was Josiah Wedgwood, wanting an effective trade route for his potteries, but the venture also helped develop the Midlands' coal, iron, steel and stone industries, as well as creating new markets for the farmers along the route. The link with the Coventry Canal at Fradley, in 1790, opened a lucrative route to London via the Oxford Canal and the Thames, and transhipment warehouses and workers' cottages sprang up around the busy junction.

Leaving the car park, turn left past the **Laughing Duck** café. Walk on to a bridge overlooking Junction Lock on the Trent & Mersey Canal. Cross and turn back along the opposite bank. After a few yards, you can detour into Fradley Pool Nature Reserve, taking a path on the left, which loops around the northern shore of the reservoir before leading back to the canal, just a little farther along.

The pool was constructed as a small reservoir to feed the canal and has become a focus for plentiful wildlife, including several species of water and woodland birds as well as pipistrelle and Daubenton's bats.

Carry on beside the canal past another lock to meet the main lane. Cross to the ongoing towpath. Walk on for 1¼ miles (2km), going by another couple of locks before passing beneath the main road outside Alrewas. The canal winds on around the edge of the town, past Bagnall Lock and under a couple of road bridges, before reaching a final lock above a brief encounter with the River Trent. Just a little farther on, bridges take you across the outflow from Alrewas mill stream and then the River

Fradley Junction

Trent itself. Canal traffic follows the river downstream for some 200 yards before branching off onto the continuing canal, the water levels balanced by a weir across the river just beyond **A**.

Although there had been a flour mill on the site since medieval times, Alrewas mill was rebuilt towards the end of the 18th century as a cotton mill. During the 19th century it was repurposed to produce wire and needles as well as flour, and then later to grind animal feed before it finally closed during the 1970s. It has since been refurbished as living accommodation.

Return along the towpath to Church Road bridge (No. 46), branching off as you approach to the road above. Walk over the bridge and take the next right into Post Office Road. At the bottom go right again along Main Street. Nearing the canal, leave left along a passage that runs between houses to a recreation field. Cross to the cricket field boundary and follow it right into the corner, from which a gravel path leads out onto the end of a street. Go right, but then turn off just before the canal on a track behind houses and beneath the main road.

Entering a field **B**, go left beside the road embankment. Reaching the corner, swing right and then left with the field boundary, continuing ahead beyond the next corner to the far side of the field. Emerging onto a lane, cross to the Alrewas Show Ground opposite. Bear right across the corner, pass through the hedge and maintain direction across the next field to a footbridge spanning a ditch. Walk on by the left edge of a

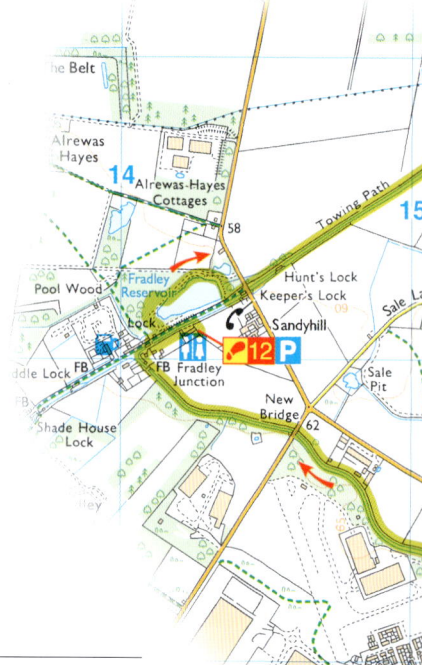

The Coventry Canal

the edge of Fradley **C**.

Follow it left around the perimeter of a small housing estate, eventually passing St Stephen's Church, an attractive building erected in 1862. Just beyond, branch left by the war memorial **D** along a lane, which leads to the Coventry Canal at Fradley Bridge. Approaching the bridge, turn off left onto the towpath and go right beneath the bridge. The canal runs for 1¼ miles (2km) to return to the Trent & Mersey Canal at Fradley Junction. There, turn right and walk back to the café and car park.

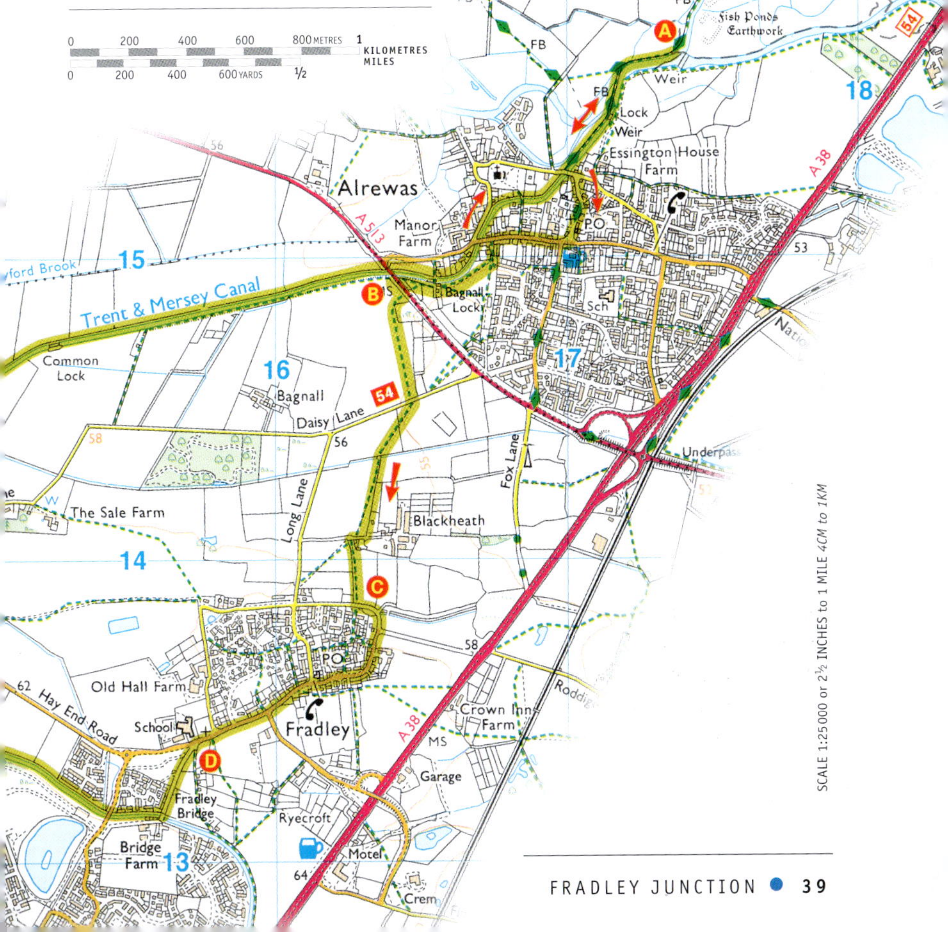

large paddock, emerging at the far end onto a track. Go right past a couple of houses and then immediately turn off left on a contained path beside them. Keep going to come out onto a lane at

FRADLEY JUNCTION • 39

walk 13

Brewood and Chillington Hall

Start: Brewood

Distance: 6½ miles (10.5km)

Height gain: 320 feet (100m)

Approximate time: 3 hours

Route terrain: Canal towpath, tracks and some lane

Parking: Car park in village

OS maps: Landranger 127 (Stafford & Telford), Explorer (242 Telford, Ironbridge & The Wrekin)

GPS waypoints:
- SJ 884 088
- Ⓐ SJ 883 082
- Ⓑ SJ 877 078
- Ⓒ SJ 874 071
- Ⓓ SJ 867 068
- Ⓔ SJ 882 066
- Ⓕ SJ 891 059

Rolling countryside, a charming country house and parkland, as well as a delightful village combine to make this walk an ideal summer's day out. It concludes with a stretch beside the Shropshire Union Canal where, more often than not, you can watch colourful narrowboats chugging by.

> **Brewood**
> Elegant Georgian buildings line the streets of the village, near to which, at Boscobel, Charles II is reputed to have hidden in an oak tree following his defeat at the Battle of Worcester. His companion, Colonel William Carless, is buried near a yew tree in the churchyard of St Mary and St Chad's.

Leaving the car park, turn left down Stafford Street. At the end, by the Lion Hotel, go right along Bargate Street to the **Bridge Inn**. Immediately before the bridge, leave through a gate on the left and walk down to the Shropshire Union Canal. Follow the towpath south to Dean's Hall Bridge (No. 12), there climbing to the track above Ⓐ.

Go over the canal and continue with the track for about ½ mile (800m). Just past a couple of large animal sheds, turn off left. Keep ahead at the next junction in front of Woolley Farm, but where the track subsequently bends right a little farther on, abandon it through a waymarked kissing-gate on the left Ⓑ. Walk away by the field edge, eventually passing out at the far end through a couple of gates onto Upper Avenue, a tree-lined grass swathe that runs from Chillington Hall. Bearing right, cut across it and leave through a gate in the trees onto a lane Ⓒ.

Turn right and walk to a junction at the end Ⓓ, from which you can see Chillington Hall. (The house is a member of HHA and only open on selected days – please enquire in advance). Go left for 250 yards, and then turn off left onto a track that later narrows to a grassy way. Carry on to its end, emerging past cottages onto a road. Cross to the narrower lane opposite, Park Lane. At a sharp bend Ⓔ, turn off right onto a track past a couple of houses and on between the fields. After some 700 yards, just beyond overhead power cables, leave through a gap in the left hedge. Walk away at the field perimeter. Reaching the corner, wind through a gap and continue with the hedge now on your left to the canal at Hunting Bridge Ⓕ.

Go over the bridge and immediately climb a metal ranch fence on the right. Drop to the towpath below and double back

Avenue Bridge

Avenue Bridge, number 10, carrying the formal tree-lined drive to Chillington Hall high above the waterway, stands out in contrast to the others passed along the way. Indeed, it is the grandest bridge on the whole of the Shropshire Union Canal and was built in 1826 to a design attributed to Thomas Telford.

beneath the bridge. Follow the canal north towards Brewood. Approaching Chillington Bridge (No. 9), the canal passes into a wooded cutting and under Avenue Bridge (No. 10), emerging some ¾ mile (1.2km) farther on to return you to Dean's Hall Bridge (No. 12) **A**. Leave the towpath just beyond the bridge, dropping to a kissing-gate. Follow the ongoing path past paddocks, over a stream and on between more fields to meet a track behind the village. Go left and immediately right beside a garage on a contained path winding through to Church Street. Follow it left and then round to the right past the church. At the top, cross diagonally into Stafford Street and return to the car park.

SCALE 1:25000 or 2½ INCHES to 1 MILE 4CM to 1KM

BREWOOD AND CHILLINGTON HALL

walk 14

Burnt Wood and Blore Heath

Start
Loggerheads

Distance
6½ miles (10.5km)

Height gain
490 feet (150m)

Approximate time
3¼ hours

Route terrain
Largely back lanes and farm tracks. Potentially very muddy near the end

Parking
Loggerheads Inn car park (public parking here)

OS maps
Landranger 127 (Stafford & Telford), Explorer 243 (Market Drayton)

GPS waypoints
- SJ 738 358
- Ⓐ SJ 742 349
- Ⓑ SJ 736 331
- Ⓒ SJ 713 339
- Ⓓ SJ 722 346

The rolling countryside, with hamlets and superb views, disguises a darker secret, for it was here in 1459 that the Battle of Blore Heath, one of the bloodiest of the Wars of the Roses, was fought-out. This walk fringes the battlefield, close to ancient Burnt Wood.

Walk along Eccleshall Road to reach pavement railings at a school in ¼ mile (400m). Virtually opposite is a hand-gate into the fir woods; use this and follow the path ahead. Keep forward over a cross-track below cables, beyond which the firs give way to old broadleaf woodland.

Burnt Wood

Burnt Wood recalls the importance of this corner of the old Forest of Blore for providing charcoal for use in the long-gone glassmaking industry in the area, first established in the late 1500s. Spread among the older oak woods are coppice stools, created by harvesting side branches on a regular cycle (around 15 years), using these to make the charcoal. Today the woodland is renowned for its abundance of butterflies and moths and is managed by the Staffordshire Wildlife Trust. Until the 1970s its secluded setting housed a sanatorium for victims of tuberculosis.

At a major junction of tracks and paths take the second-left, rising gently beside a line of tall firs (right). In time this path will pass below a run of low cables to reach a sharp-left bend. Here go ahead right on a thin path through undergrowth to reach a wood-side track at old gates Ⓐ.

Turn right, breaking free of the trees to reveal extensive views across Shropshire, while on the left a stretch of heather and gorse heath recalls the original vegetation of this area. Advance along the track to a sharp-right bend beyond a strip of woodland. Here use the stile on the left and walk beside the hedgerow; beyond a double-stile drift right to a wooded corner and a farm lane. Use the gate and walk gently uphill to reach farm buildings **B**.

Turn right on the concreted track. At the next junction go left, falling to another junction; here turn right. Pretty views emerge to the left across the deeply cut valley of little Coal Brook. Remain on the lane past the imposing buildings of the Hales Estate. As the lane bends left beyond wooded Lloyd Drumble, a level platform in the field on the left marks the site of a substantial 2nd century Roman villa and bath house, excavated in the 1960s.

At the heart of a large estate, its modern equivalent is the Georgian Hales Hall. To find this keep ahead through the estate village of Hales and turn right at the T-junction, shortly reaching St Mary's Church opposite the

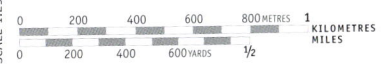

BURNT WOOD AND BLORE HEATH • 43

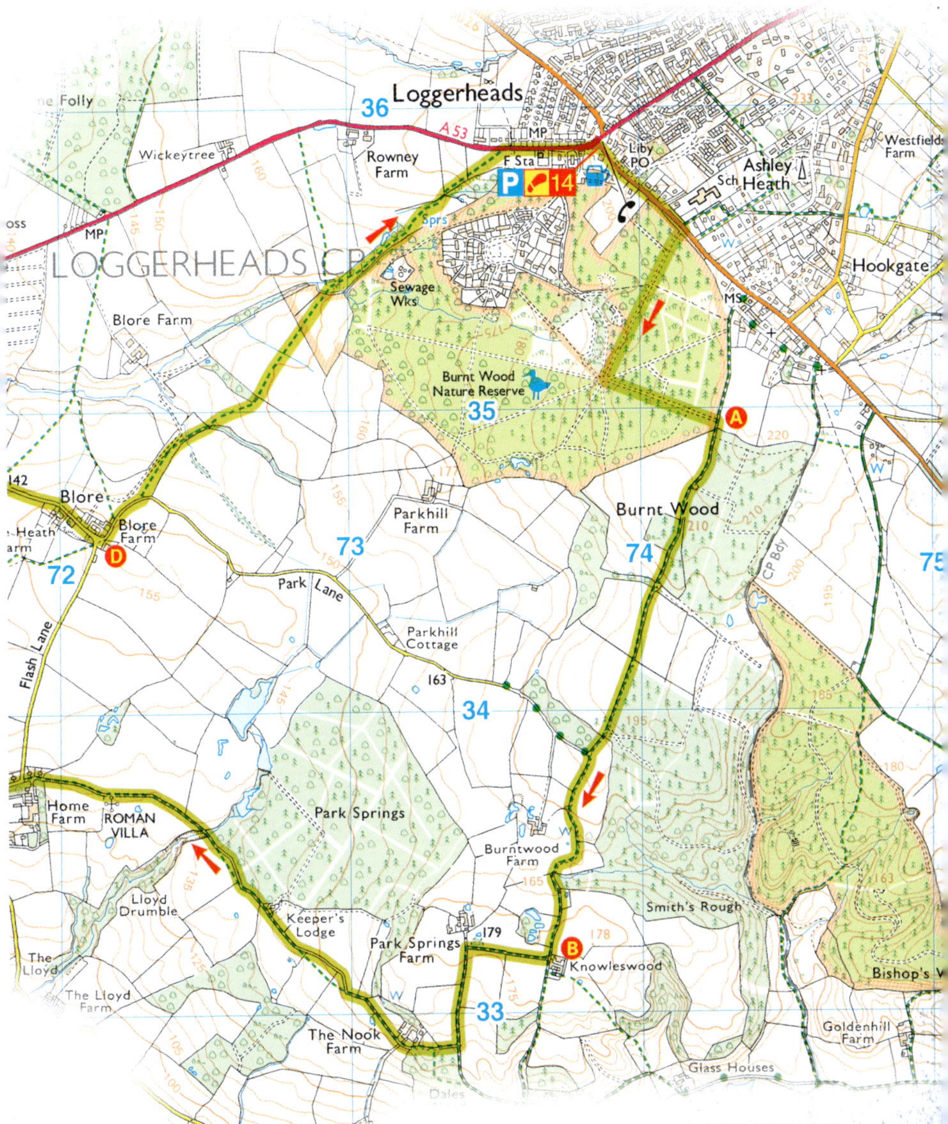

gated Hall driveway. The church dates from 1856; designed by renowned architect George Gilbert Scott, architect of St Pancras Station in London, it replaced a medieval wooden one that burned down.

Turn right at the junction **C** here, rising gently on a long straight. At the sharp left-hand bend, go through the left-hand gateway on the right and ahead to the nearby corner and waymarked stile. Climb this and turn left up a fieldside path. Use another corner stile before drifting right to a stile into a lane; beyond this is a late-medieval battlefield.

Turn right along the lane, which traces the 'High Hedge' boundary marking the front-line of the Lancastrian forces. Turn left along the 'No Through Road' **D** at Blore Farm. Before this bends right, look carefully for the Newcastle Way fingerpost on the left. Turn right within the field, picking up a well-waymarked path across fields and stiles. At the second subsequent stile, cut across the long field for the right-end of the strip of trees, then ahead again to a stile into immature woodland. Keep left at a fork; at the far end turn right past a pond, joining a muddy path past further ponds, then over a boardwalk bridge. Bear right to and through a gate, then head for a stile opposite houses. *Take particular care here in crossing the main A53 road* and turn right to return to **Loggerheads Inn**.

> **Blore Heath**
>
> The Battle of Blore Heath, fought on 23 September 1459, was the first major battle of the Wars of the Roses, when over 3,000 were killed and the Lancastrians routed by their Yorkist foes. Their commander, Lord Audley, was among the dead; a memorial to him and the other victims stands in a field at the heart of the conflict.

Old coppiced oaks in Burnt Wood

Three Shire Heads

walk 15

As its name suggests, Three Shire Heads marks the meeting of three different counties, Staffordshire, Derbyshire and Cheshire, the boundaries marked by the River Dane and an unnamed tributary stream, which come together over separate waterfalls. This lonely spot was also a junction of moorland packhorse routes along which both goods and raw materials were laboriously trekked throughout the year, the cross-country motorways of their day.

Start
Wildboarclough

Distance
6¼ miles (10.1km)

Height gain
1,245 feet (380m)

Approximate time
3½ hours

Route terrain
Moorland paths and tracks, some lane

Parking
Car park at start

OS maps
Landranger 118 (Stoke on Trent & Macclesfield) and 119 (Buxton, Matlock, Bakewell & Dovedale), Explorer OL24 (The Peak District, White Peak)

GPS waypoints
- SJ 987 698
- Ⓐ SJ 997 699
- Ⓑ SK 001 707
- Ⓒ SK 009 685
- Ⓓ SK 002 681
- Ⓔ SJ 995 685
- Ⓕ SJ 982 685

Head from the car park over a bridge towards Clough House Farm and bend up left to the lane. Cross to a gate opposite and follow the ongoing track up the valley, signed to The Cat and Fiddle Inn. Shortly, switch banks and climb beside a pretty, wooded section of Cumberland Brook. Ignore the later track off left and carry on beyond the trees, before long approaching a small but splendid waterfall.

Through a gate and stile beside the fall Ⓐ, leave the main trail at a footpath sign to head up beside a tributary stream. The path eventually crosses below another small fall, climbing out a few yards beyond to a junction above it. Keep ahead, now on a broader path, which then winds left and right through a broken wall to continue beside it. Through a gate, keep going above the gully, soon crossing the stream. Stream and path then part company, the way now rising more easily across the open moor to a crossing track Ⓑ.

Go right, the way signed towards Three Shire Heads. It gently descends to Danebower Hollow and ultimately emerges through a gate onto the main A54 road. Cross to a stile opposite behind the crash barrier. The path is signed down a steep bank, but it is easier to slant left to a lower track and then

> **Danebower** Although now deserted save for the occasional birdwatcher, Danebower echoed to the sounds of industry during the 19th century. The quarries either side of the river were worked for gritstone, which was used as roofing flags, kerbs and lintels. The tall ventilation chimney was part of a separate enterprise, the Danebower Colliery, which lay beside the river just downstream. A stone flue connected it to the furnace, sited a little farther down the hill, while the entrance to the mine is by the river. It was worked from around the end of the 18th century until it finally closed in about 1925.

double back right. Watch for the path then branching off left down to an isolated chimney that served the Danebower Colliery. From the chimney, drop to a lower path that carries on through a gate and down the valley. Later through a kissing-gate, the way slips behind a fence, crossing side streams before swinging away to a stile. Go left over a bridge and continue on a better path above the river, eventually reaching a bridge at Three Shire Heads **C**.

The onward path remains on the west bank, rising above the stream before turning round the southern flank of Cut-thorn Hill. Ignore a later path leaving left, and walk on to emerge onto a narrow lane beside Cut-thorn Cottage **D**.

Turn right, but then leave through a gate immediately beyond the cottage for a path across the moor. Although apparently heading for a gate on the skyline, watch for it swinging left to meet the wall farther along. Through a broken gap and then over a stile, ignore a path signed off left and instead keep ahead, shortly meeting the main road again **E**.

Cross to a stile opposite and continue across the moor, a series of walkways leading to a gate. Keep going, passing a small barn on your left and then joining a wall down to a gate at the edge of woodland. A rough track drops through the trees to a lane at the bottom. Go down right and then keep left past a junction by Crag Hall; there is a glimpse of it lower down the lane. Bend left below the church and cross Clough Brook to another junction.

Walk left, but after a few yards, turn off sharp right along a private road **F** that climbs back along the valley side. In late spring, the woods below are full of bluebells and there is a fine view across the valley. Up to the left is Shutlingsloe – The Cheshire Matterhorn, which has been a landmark on the skyline since Cut-thorn Hill. At a fork, branch off right to contour round the hill past Banktop and then a barn.

> **Wildboarclough**
>
> During the 19th century, the fast-flowing Clough Brook was harnessed to power a textile mill for both spinning and printing of carpets and calico. The first mill was constructed in 1793 and two others followed on the site, with cottages being built for the workers. The mill owner, George Palfreyman, built Crag Hall for himself and Crag Lodge for his manager. The mill buildings were largely demolished in the 1950s, but the imposing office building with its attractive blue-faced clock survives. After the mill closed, the ground floor was occupied by the local post office and postmaster's house, while the upper storey served as the village hall.

Three Shire Heads

The way gradually falls beyond, bringing you back to the lane. Cross to a bridge opposite and walk up behind Clough House Farm. Turn in to the yard and go right. At the far end, swing left back to the car park. ●

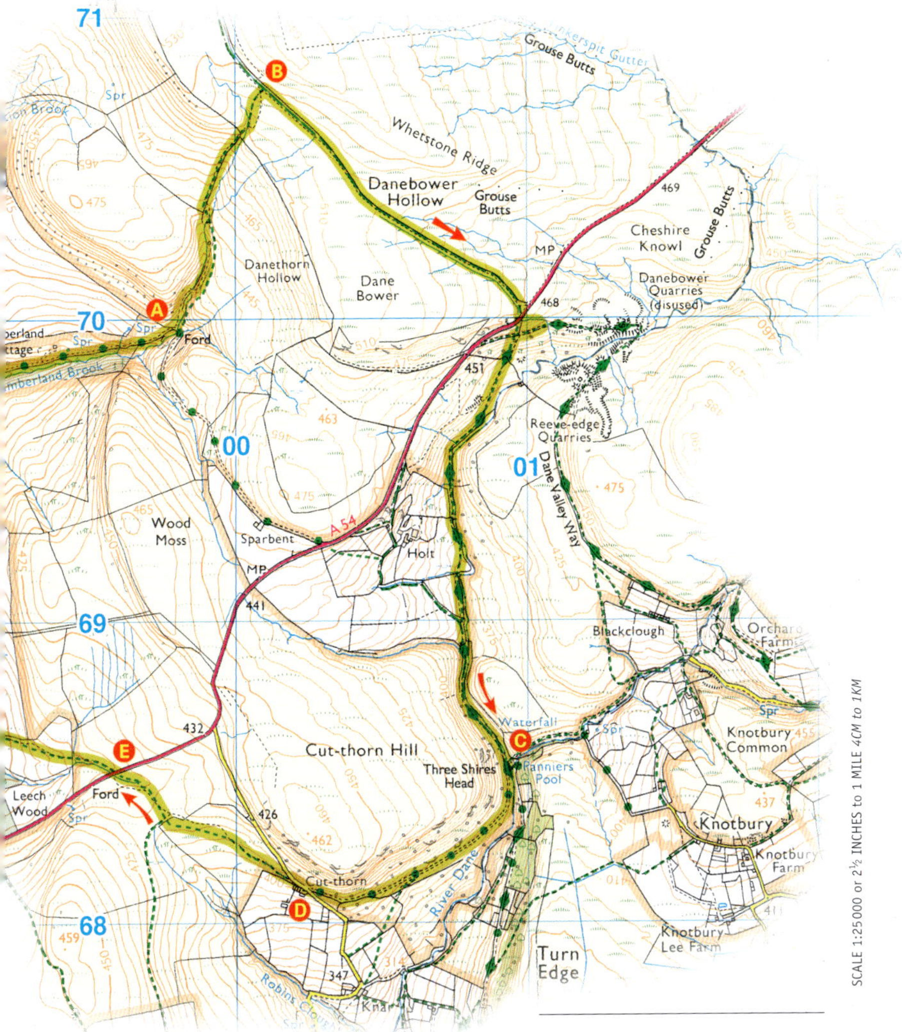

SCALE 1:25 000 or 2½ INCHES to 1 MILE 4CM to 1KM

THREE SHIRE HEADS ● 47

walk 16 *The Roaches*

Start
Roaches Gate on Roach Road

Distance
6½ miles (10.5km)

Height gain
1,180 feet (360m)

Approximate time
3½ hours

Route terrain
Moorland paths and lane

Parking
Roadside parking at start

OS maps
Landranger 118 (Stoke on Trent & Macclesfield) and 119 (Buxton, Matlock, Bakewell & Dovedale), Explorer OL24 (The Peak District, White Peak)

GPS waypoints
- SK 004 621
- Ⓐ SK 007 620
- Ⓑ SK 012 632
- Ⓒ SK 016 638
- Ⓓ SK 006 645
- Ⓔ SJ 995 644
- Ⓕ SK 005 625

Lying close to the western edge of the Peak District National Park and overlooking the Meerbrook valley, The Roaches and Hen Cloud are perhaps the most visually dramatic rock features of the Staffordshire Moorlands. The soaring escarpment, a prominent landmark of the area, is both an exhilarating walk and magnet for climbers who come to pit their skills against the rugged gritstone crags.

> **Rock Hall Cottage**
>
> Tucked below the cliff is the Don Whillans Memorial Hut. Built in 1862 around a natural crevice in the cliff and lacking any amenity other than a natural spring, it was originally used as a gamekeeper's cottage. Before that the cave had been inhabited by Bess Bowyer, who reputedly harboured smugglers and deserters and lived to be nearly 100 years old. When the Swythamley estate was sold off in the 1970s, Doug Moller bought the dwelling and lived there with his wife until 1990. The Peak District Authority then offered the place to the British Mountaineering Council, who had started a fund to establish a climbing hut in memory of Don Whillans. An apt choice as it was here that the 18-year-old Whillans first teamed up with Joe Brown, and so started his career as one of Britain's truly great climbers.

Leave the lane through a gate by the bus lay-by (Roaches Gate). Keep with the uphill path ahead, passing through a gate onto a col dividing The Roaches from Hen Cloud. A little farther along, a path off through a gate on the right Ⓐ leads across a field and on to the top of Hen Cloud.

Return to the col and go right, signed to Upper Hulme. At first, the way still gains height, before gently falling across open moor. Eventually, pass through a gate to join a track from Summerhill and follow it away to the left. Keep ahead as a second track joins, ultimately meeting a lane Ⓑ.

Walk right and then later, keep left past a junction. A little farther along, bear off on a track to Hazel Barrow. Pass between the buildings and then swing right at the end along a grass track that returns you to the lane. Go left.

After 50 yards, abandon it over a stile on the left Ⓒ. Walk down beside a ditch to reach a gate on the right. A rough path leads to a second gate, the way now dogging a fence across the moor. Entering a corner cul-de-sac, leave over a stile and follow the wall right behind buildings at Blackbank to a stile.

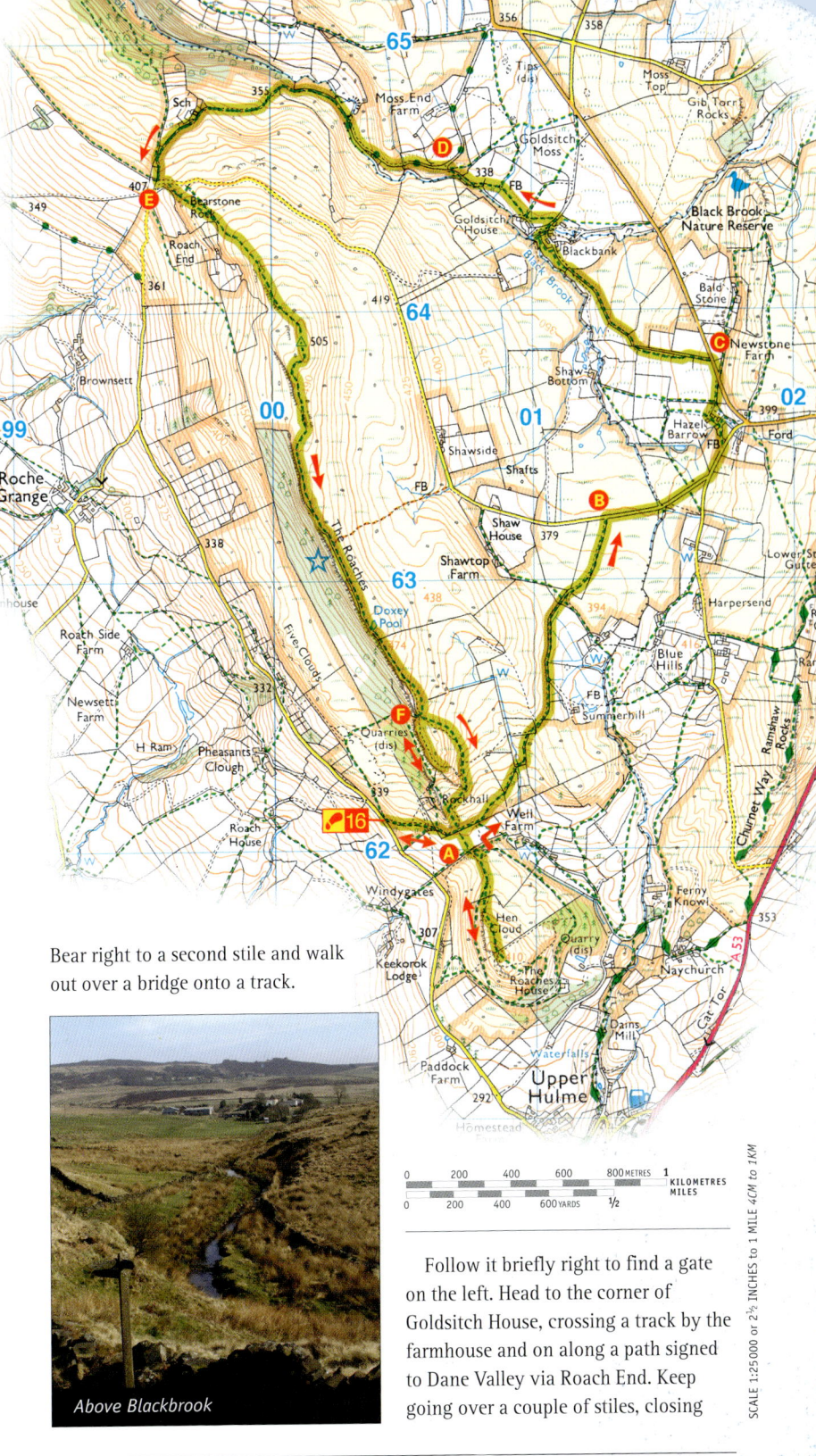

Bear right to a second stile and walk out over a bridge onto a track.

Above Blackbrook

Follow it briefly right to find a gate on the left. Head to the corner of Goldsitch House, crossing a track by the farmhouse and on along a path signed to Dane Valley via Roach End. Keep going over a couple of stiles, closing

> **Doxey Pool** There's more than one remote pool in these lonely hills said to be haunted by mermaids. The one here is home to Ginny Greenteeth, who, one day long ago, slipped and drowned while out walking in fog. And now, when the mist is down, her lingering spirit tries to entice the unwary into sharing her watery fate.

with Black Brook on the left. As the valley narrows, the path rises to a junction **D**. Go ahead towards Roach End, later crossing a bridge. The path then begins to rise onto heath above the stream and shortly turns away towards a building that soon appears on the skyline. Walk on to join a roughly metalled track that climbs to the lane at Roach End **E**.

Cross to the path opposite, and, as you gain height along The Roaches ridge, pause to enjoy the retrospective view, which includes Shutlingsloe (the Cheshire Matterhorn), Sutton Common – identified by a tall transmitter mast – and The Cloud. The way rises steadily to a trig column marking the high point, which gives a superb panorama that on a clear day extends across Cheshire to Snowdon, while to the north is Winter Hill, part of the West Pennine moors. Beyond, the path gently falls along the top of the spectacular cliff past a succession of outcrops and boulders that have been weathered into striking shapes. After passing a small tarn, Doxey Pool, the path eventually reaches a junction with a path coming up through a gully on the right **F**.

The easy way back is to the left, while the gully path descends to the foot of the cliff and then winds back past the Don Whillans Memorial Hut. First, however, for more impressive views wander on along the path ahead; it leads onto the rocky southern point of The Roaches ridge. A scrambling path drops off left through the boulders just before the end, but it is easier to return to the junction by the gully and double back right. The way falls more gradually below the rocks to the col passed at the beginning of the walk. There is then another chance to scale Hen Cloud before heading back down to the lane.

Hen Cloud

Dovedale

From its source at Dove Head, below Axe Edge in the Northern Peak, the River Dove flows through a succession of lonely dales before reaching the best-known section, which is actually named for the river. For many, Dovedale is the Peak District and this superb walk, starting close by the famous Izaak Walton Hotel, not only takes you right through the spectacular gorge, but also scales the hills of its western flank to give a wider perspective of the valley's position within the surrounding landscape.

walk 17

Start
Dovedale

Distance
6½ miles (10.5km)

Height gain
1,265 feet (385m)

Approximate time
3½ hours

Route terrain
Field and riverside paths, some lane

Parking
Car park at start

OS maps
Landrangers 119 (Buxton, Matlock, Bakewell & Dovedale), Explorer OL24 (The Peak District, White Peak)

GPS waypoints
- SK 146 509
- Ⓐ SK 138 512
- Ⓑ SK 133 523
- Ⓒ SK 129 531
- Ⓓ SK 131 542
- Ⓔ SK 139 546

A natural wonder

Eighteenth-century landscape artists such as Thomas Smith and Romantic writers including Charles Cotton and Izaak Walton began the popularisation of Dovedale, inspiring the gentry to experience its awesome beauty for themselves. And indeed it was truly breathtaking, for the gaunt rock pinnacles and soaring, naked cliffs could intimidate frail hearts used to more genteel visions of nature. Later, the advent of the railways (Thorpe Cloud Station was less than 2 miles/3.2km away) opened the pleasures to many more, who appreciated the joy of the countryside; a welcome escape from the hardships of working life. Now protected by the National Trust, Dovedale's loveliness continues to attract today's visitors and the dale more than justifies its inclusion as one of the Seven Natural Wonders of the UK.

From the Dovedale car park by the toilets, start along the riverside path. Reaching a gauge station, just upstream, turn off left, crossing the drive to a path signed to Ilam. Climb gently away at the fringe of scrub above the trees. Seen out to the left is the Izaak Walton Hotel, while the view ahead is to Ilam and its hall. Eventually levelling, the path continues through a gate across the slope of Bunster Hill. Later on, through another gate, pass a stile on the left and carry on to a fork.

Take the right-hand branch, rising steeply to a grassy col on the southern ridge of Bunster Hill Ⓐ, from which there is an impressive view down to Ilam in the valley below. Walk over the crest and swing right on a faint path that contours the hill's steep western flank. Take care over outcrops of limestone, which can be slippery when wet. Beyond a gate, the way runs across more gently sloping pasture to a stile in the far-left corner. Carry on, keeping well right of trees and then above an old quarry pit. Mounting a stile left of a gateway, continue over

Dove Holes

a track to find a final stile onto Ilam Moor Lane B .

Turn right, up the hill. After a little over ½ mile (800m), beyond the crest, watch for a gated track off right, beside which is a signed squeeze stile into the corner of a field C . Head diagonally out to another stile in the opposite corner, over which, follow the left wall down to a second stile. Again strike out diagonally to a small gate in the distant corner and then walk on by the left wall. Through yet another squeeze, head out to join a wall on your left. Stick with it at the edge of the next field and then cross the bottom of the subsequent pasture to a gate and three-way signpost. Take the path ahead, joining another wall on your left. Keep going beyond its corner and across a final field to meet a track, Pasture Lane D .

Follow it right, but at a bend, go ahead over a stile by a gate. Follow the field edge from field to field, crossing out at the bottom into the fold of a dale. Continue down, emerging beside a cottage onto a lane at the edge of Milldale. Walk right into the village, bearing right again at the bottom, to find the National Trust's information barn and Viator Bridge, a medieval packhorse bridge E .

Cross to the other bank and head downstream. After some ¾ mile (1.2km), just beyond a path off to Alsop en le Dale, the way passes beneath the impressive Dove Holes, the largest of which is 33 feet (10m) high and twice as wide at the cave's mouth. A little farther downstream, the river bends past the foot of Hall Dale and the imposing freestanding pillar of Ilam Rock, while on this bank is Pickering Tor. Lower down, the narrowing gorge forces the path along a causeway but when it widens again, look up left to see a natural arch and Reynard's Cave, which can be reached by a side path doubling back just beyond. Farther on, another series of pillars is known as Tissington Spires. Reaching a fork, take the higher path, which climbs to a splendid viewpoint known as Lover's Leap. Beyond, as the path falls back to the river, look for fossils embedded in the steps. The valley then opens as it approaches a sharp bend of the river at the foot of Lin Dale. You can cross the water there on the stepping stones or else continue a little farther downstream to a bridge. It is then just a short walk back by the river to the car park.

Lover's Leap

The Victorians were masters of embellishing nature with legend; why should fact get in the way of a good story? At Lover's Leap, a despairing maiden supposedly threw herself from the cliff when she learned that her lover was dead. But her fall was broken by a tree and she recovered to learn that he too was still alive. Less lucky was the Reverend Dean Langton, who after picnicking with friends, steered his horse up the steep hillside to explore Reynard's Cave. His mount lost its footing and the good clergyman fell to his death.

walk 18

Grindon and the River Hamps

Start: Grindon

Distance: 6¾ miles (10.9km)

Height gain: 1,025 feet (310m)

Approximate time: 3½ hours

Route terrain: Tracks and field paths

Parking: Car park at start

OS maps: Landrangers 119 (Buxton, Matlock, Bakewell & Dovedale), Explorer OL24 (The Peak District, White Peak)

GPS waypoints:
- 🖍 SK 085 545
- Ⓐ SK 085 542
- Ⓑ SK 083 519
- Ⓒ SK 080 516
- Ⓓ SK 093 515
- Ⓔ SK 103 539
- Ⓕ SK 096 539

A lovely walk over the 'green hill' of Grindon, which gives a panorama to the hills in the south, returning through the deep, narrow valley of the River Hamps along the track of the former Manifold Light Railway. There is a final, but pretty climb back to the village, which reveals views to the confluence with the Manifold, overlooked by Beeston Tor. Grindon's pub has sadly long gone, but The Red Lion lies beside the route at Waterfall.

Grindon church

With its tall spire, All Saints' is known as the 'Cathedral of the Moorlands' and was founded as a chapel of ease to Ilam in the 11th century. Reminders of that early building are there in the Saxon font, a window panel of medieval glass and a pair of massive charnel coffins, once used to store old bones unearthed when reopening graves. An embroidered memorial remembers eight men who died in 1947 when a Halifax of 47 Squadron crashed on Grindon Moor. An exceptionally severe winter and deep snow had left these upland villages completely cut off for several weeks and the plane was attempting to drop much-needed food supplies. Unfortunately, as the plane approached, the weather closed in and, in trying to locate the drop zone, it hit the ground killing six crew members and two news photographers. Ironically, the road to Leek was reopened later the same day. Outside the church, a pillar has the curious inscription, 'Lord of the Manor of Grindon established his right to this rindle at the Staffordshire Assizes on 17 March 1862'. A rindle is a local word for a stream that flows only after rain, but why the Lord of the Manor felt the need to assert his right in such a way is a mystery.

🖍 Out of the car park behind the church, walk left past a small green and turn right. Keep left past the next junction, but as the lane then bends in front of the restored village pin fold where stray livestock were held Ⓐ, go ahead on a lesser lane. Follow it past occasional farms for almost a mile (1.6km) to its end at Oldfields Farm. Pass through the yard, winding out at the far end to leave along a field track by a wall on the right. Through a gate, bear right across pasture and pass through a couple more gates to carry on beside a wall on the left. The way shortly develops as a hollow way, Slade Lane, and continues down the hill.

Emerging onto a lane at the bottom Ⓑ, go right and then

left. After fording a stream, look for a path on the right winding up through scrub into a rough field. Climb away left towards the church, where a squeeze gate leads into the graveyard. Pass right of the church to find an exit gate in the corner. Head straight out across another rough field, leaving at the far side over a stile just right of cottages onto a lane opposite the **Red Lion Inn C**.

Turn left to the village green and double back left by a red telephone box along a drive. Beside a cottage at the end, go through a squeeze stile on the right. Head out, passing between farm buildings at the far side onto another lane. Cross to a squeeze diagonally opposite and head out past a slurry tank. Over a stile follow the trod ahead, descending along a

GRINDON AND THE RIVER HAMPS • 55

> **The River Hamps**
>
> The source of the river lies high on Merriton Law below the Mermaid Inn, but after flowing south for eight miles (13km) is turned back on itself below Caldon Low to run north through a deep gorge to meet the River Manifold. Curiously, Warslow Brook, which has its source barely half a mile (800m) away, cuts east in an almost direct line to the Manifold. The name of the Hamps is said to come from an ancient English word meaning 'Summer Dry', and refers to the fact that it invariably disappears at Waterhouses during summer to leave a dry riverbed all the way through the gorge. The underground stream takes a completely different course and resurges to join the Manifold at Hamps Spring by Ilam.

fold to find a gate in the bottom corner. Walk on over a bridge, but ignore the stile ahead and instead turn right beside the stream. Lower down, at a couple of stiles, take the one ahead beside a gate and continue down a long pasture to emerge at the bottom onto the Manifold Way **D**.

Follow the trail left beside the River Hamps and carry on along the deep, meandering valley for a couple of miles (3.2km), occasionally crossing and re-crossing the river. Eventually, beyond the National Trust's Old Soles Wood, the valley begins to open out and there is a view to the impressive cliff face of Beeston Tor ahead. Passing a small campsite, look for a bridleway signed through a gate on the left to Lees Barn **E**.

Marked by occasional wayposts, a winding path climbs the scrubby hillside. Approaching a field gate, bear left beside the fence above the valley. Through a bridle gate, continue by the fence and then a wall. The way develops as a track that comes out onto the bend of a lane. A little way farther up the hill, a path leaves through a gate on the left **F**. Walk away beside the wall over the crest. After passing through a couple of gates, turn right to gain height along the base of a grassy fold. Continue up across a succession of enclosures, eventually entering the corner of a field. Bear left behind Buckfurlong Farm and maintain the line across a couple of paddocks beyond to meet a track. Go left past a farm and behind cottages. At the end, go right to come out onto a lane. Turn right and then first left, heading up past houses back to the church and car park.

Beeston Tor

Milwich and Sandon Park

The heart of Staffordshire is rolling, well-watered countryside dappled with small villages and hamlets. From peaceful Milwich, paths undulate to reach the landscaped parkland surrounding Sandon Hall before skimming past secluded Gayton to return to the start and a welcoming village inn.

walk 19

Start
Milwich Community Hall (opposite the Green Man pub)

Distance
7¼ miles (11.7km)

Height gain
550 feet (170m)

Approximate time
3½ hours

Route terrain
Field paths, farm tracks, lanes. Gentle climbs, with some muddy sections

Parking
Community Hall car park

OS maps
Landranger 127 (Stafford & Telford), Explorers 244 (Cannock Chase & Chasewater) and 258 (Stoke-on-Trent & Newcastle-under-Lyme)

GPS waypoints
- SJ 971 323
- Ⓐ SJ 956 295
- Ⓑ SJ 976 284
- Ⓒ SJ 979 297
- Ⓓ SJ 977 312

Turn by **The Green Man** pub for Sandon and Stafford. Just past the last bungalow on the left, use the signed footpath to the church. The treble bell in the peal at All Saints Church in Milwich was cast in 1409 and is the seventh oldest bell in England still in use. Walk past the tower to the hand-gate and turn right, over a stile and ahead to a double stile beneath the line of trees beyond the brook. Past these go half-left to a stile in-line with two distant poplars. Over another stile, use the nearby hedge gap and then aim for the farmhouse on the skyline. Take a tractor bridge and look right for a gap beside an old stump; aim then left of the ancient in-field oak, gaining the ridgetop just left of a small reservoir cap.

Turn right over the stile and walk past the reservoir. Extensive views stretch left to Cannock Chase and right across the rolling hills of East Staffordshire. After the second stile (beside woods), turn left down the sloping pasture, aiming for the obvious farm track leading into the distance; join this by crossing the farm road via a waymarked stile. Beyond a gateway, this hedgeside track passes a neck of trees; here head half-right over a hedgerow stile and drop towards the far-right bottom corner, 100 yards up from which a tricky gate is waymarked. Use this, cross the nearby brook and turn right along a marshy pasture. Use two stiles up from the gas pipeline marker post; then drift left to the driveway right of the brick cottage. Walk this into the parkland here at Sandon Park, presently reaching a black-and-white farmhouse and a junction Ⓐ.

The way is left over the cattle-grid, but first divert right to visit the hilltop All Saints Church, parish church to Sandon village and the huge estate, seat of the Earls of Harrowby. Return to cross the grid and follow the drive past the substantial old moat (where the medieval Sandon Hall stood). Before reaching the ornate lodge-house on the left, use the waymarked stile on your right and aim to pass the right corner of the spinney ahead.

Winter sunshine on Gayton Brook

Walk the field path well above the pond, putting woodland on your right as the pasture crests. Just past the small group of pines, drift downhill and left, roughly in-line just left of the distant Rugeley Power Station chimneys. Cross the slope-foot farm drive and use a stile, putting a hedge on your right. Beyond a corner stile cross the brick culvert and head right to the far end of the copse. Look 50 yards beyond for stiles and a plank bridge. Tackle these and head slightly right across the heart of two pastures to a gate/stile right of a pond. The left-edge of the next pasture leads to a stile and nearby footbridge; cross and bear left beside Gayton Brook.

At the huge hollow tree **B** bear left, remaining close to the brook over two stiles then use another footbridge. Cross the nearby farm track and stile, aiming half-right to a stile/gate into a tarred lane. Turn left; at the fork keep right alongside a brook.

At a sharp left bend use the way-marked stile **C** on the right; turn left along the field edge and over a line of four well-waymarked stiles. The fourth is beside a concrete cattle-trough; turn right to climb a nearby stile, then left beside the hedge. Cut the corner to a skyline stile, then head half-right, soon dropping to stiles left of a pond; continue to a lane at Coton Mill Farm **D**. Turn right and cross the river. Enter the farmyard, left, and look right for the stile beside a hollybush. Go left along the field edge to another stile, then

Sandon Hall

Glimpsed through the trees, Victorian Sandon Hall is a private residence now used as a wedding and function venue. On your left the folly is a belvedere tower originally at Trentham Hall (near Stoke-on-Trent) and is the only remaining part of that; designed by Sir Charles Barry, architect of the Houses of Parliament and moved here in 1912 when Trentham was demolished.

ahead with the brook on your left to a stile above a gate. Head for the far-left corner (not the footbridge), from where keep the brook on your left to reach the garden of The Green Man pub.

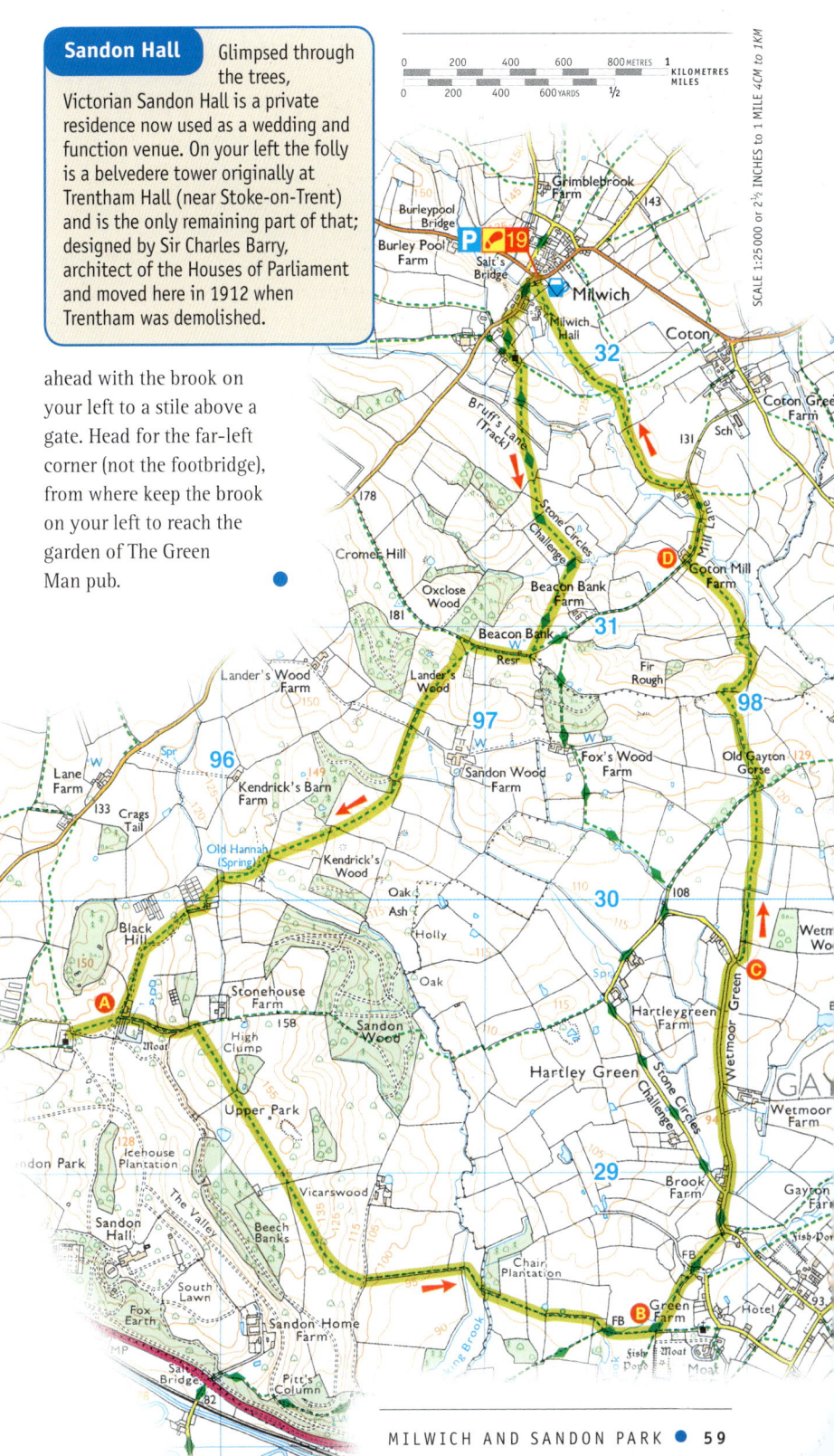

MILWICH AND SANDON PARK • 59

walk 20

Ellastone, Calwich and Wootton Park

Start	Ellastone
Distance	7¼ miles (11.7km)
Height gain	730 feet (225m)
Approximate time	3½ hours
Route terrain	Generally firm paths and tracks. May be very muddy at **A** and near the end. Lots of hills and descents; take care with routefinding between **C** and **D**
Parking	Car park off Church Lane by village institute
OS maps	Landranger 119 (Buxton & Matlock), Explorer 259 (Derby)
GPS waypoints	SK 116 434 **A** SK 129 433 **B** SK 121 439 **C** SK 105 449 **D** SK 095 435 **E** SK 100 422

Discover the bucolic countryside which inspired the Victorian writer George Eliot to set her novel Adam Bede *here. Ellastone was a backwater in the farming county of 'Loamshire'; it remains today a beautiful, secluded area of hamlets and woodlands between the Weaver Hills and the River Dove. Handel, too, produced his most famous masterpiece during a stay beside the River Dove here.*

Return to the main road and turn right, passing the old **Duncombe Arms** pub. Turn left on Dove Street. At the bend turn left at the old gatehouse along an estate road which threads through old parkland, presently arriving at barns and the ruins of Calwich Hall's stables.

A literary past

Tranquil now, there was a copper-smelting mill at Ellastone in the 1700s. George Eliot (Mary Ann Evans) based her fictional 'Hayslope' village on Ellastone; she knew the village through having relations living here. Just along the Dove Valley stood Calwich Hall. The mansion itself was demolished in 1935; it stood on the site of Calwich Abbey, a medieval Augustinian Priory-turned country house where Handel is believed to have composed his *Messiah* in 1741.

At the ruins, use a waymarked field gate (left) **A** and turn back-left through the foot of snowdrop woods to a kissing-gate into pasture. Head slightly right, presently using a gate-side stile, then half-right to a stile onto a road. Cross and bear left at the redundant stile within the field, cutting half-left to the far bottom corner. Take a stile through a stone wall and curl left to a plank footbridge. Waymarks guide you up towards imposing

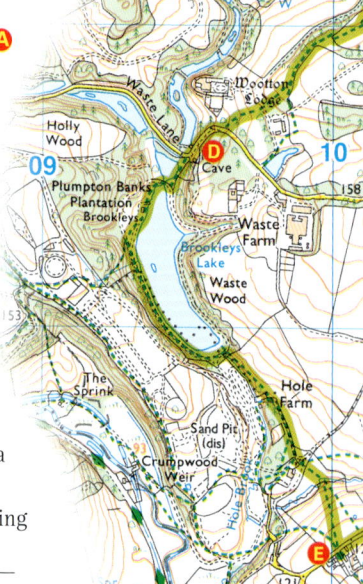

iron gates, to the left of which is a stile into a lane.

Go left a few paces, then right up the tarred lane **B**. Past a cattle-grid this becomes a field road through old parkland. At the secluded cottage, drift left to a gate beneath a fir and then ahead on the rougher track. Off to the left are glimpses of imposing Wootton Hall while ahead are the shapely Weaver Hills. Beyond a gate; stay with the lane past cottages to reach a green-centred junction. Fork left through the hamlet of Wootton. Keep left at the notice board; then right past the phone box, dropping through a cutting to the main road; turn left **C**.

In 200 yards; just past the cottage, take the waymarked field gate on the right, joining a sunken grassy track beside woodland. As this fades left, head half-right to a tumbled wall. A waymark post at the far end indicates a stile into trees. Keep ahead; in 100 yards keep right at the fork, entering woodland via a tall metal hand-gate. The marked path drops down through these firwoods to a stile into a rough lane. Go straight over, alongside

ELLASTONE, CALWICH AND WOOTTON PARK • 61

Wootton Lodge

reaches a lane through a door in the estate wall. Turn right and drop to the sharp-right bend; here use a gap stile, left D.

Walk to a footbridge and road across the neck between two lakes. Cross this and drop down the steps, left, to find a lakeside path, which passes by a boathouse, becoming a tarred lane. At the nearby junction, look right for the waymarked path into the woods. Take this; in 50 paces go left on a lesser path, parallel to the lane down to your left. At the far end, cross the lane half-left, picking up the waymarked path beneath firs below a 'No Entry' sign. Cross a footbridge and take the stile upslope on the right; a woodland path emerges beyond stiles onto a lane. Keep ahead to a barrier. Climb the stile, left and then a further stile beyond another tarred lane. Head half-right to find a narrow footbridge over a brook. From the higher stile, aim right of the solitary oak to a stile into a lane E.

Turn left through the hamlet of Prestwood. At the T-junction use the stile ahead, drifting half-left to a stile at the ridge-crest. Use this; beyond the holly hedge head half-left again to a field corner stile into a lane. Take the stile diagonally opposite, dropping ahead-left to a stile in the bottom corner. Cross the foot of the pasture to another stile; head slightly right to a further stile and brook, then make your way to a stile left of the new stone house. The road beyond is close to Ellastone church. ●

woodland on your right.

Cross straight over the tarred driveway, gradually bending right to join the second (middle) driveway just right of old oaks. Turn right, walking to the point just before gates through a boundary wall. Fork left within the pasture, wall to your right. At the corner use the tall metal hand-gate, then obey the waymark arrow left on a woodland path. This reaches a waymarked fork at the edge of the woods; turn right and walk beside the wooded bank-top, shortly passing just right of a vast old tree and dropping to the driveway to Wootton Lodge a little below estate buildings. The magnificent Elizabethan mansion is at the heart of an estate belonging to the JCB Company.

Cross directly over the drive, keeping well left of the weeping beech and stand of trees. Look diligently beyond the greensward for a waymark arrow beneath tall, slender firs, pointing the way beside a rhododendron and then right, along a narrow, railed path, which

Gnosall Heath

Three of the 'Great Ages' in the development of this country's transport are brought together on this fine ramble centred on the North Staffordshire village of Gnosall Heath; first-century Roman roads, 18th-century canals and 19th-century railways.

walk 21

Start
Car park off minor lane, south off A518, west of Gnosall Heath

Distance
7½ miles (12.1km)

Height gain
420 feet (130m)

Approximate time
3½ hours

Route terrain
Tracks, towpath and field paths, some lane

Parking
Small parking area beside the Stafford to Newport Greenway, 1 mile (1.6km) west of Gnosall Heath

OS maps
Landranger 127 (Stafford & Telford), Explorers 242 (Telford, Ironbridge & The Wrekin) and 243 (Market Drayton)

GPS waypoints
- SJ 806 201
- Ⓐ SJ 802 189
- Ⓑ SJ 811 180
- Ⓒ SJ 822 171
- Ⓓ SJ 828 164
- Ⓔ SJ 817 205

Climb to the former railway track behind the parking area and follow it right, crossing a bridge over the lane. After 700 yards, before reaching another bridge, turn off left to find a parallel path. Go right, gently rising around the base of a wooded hill to emerge onto a crossing track. Walk left for some 200 yards to a fork and bear right. Keep ahead as another track joins to meet a junction opposite the drive of a house. Go right and then swing left, walking out to a lane Ⓐ.

Cross to a stile opposite and head away, joining the right hedge. Continue beyond its corner to a stile in the opposite boundary. Keep going across a second field, making for a stile towards the right-hand end of the far hedge. Walk on by the left fence to a second stile and head out across the field parallel to the left hedge. Climb another stile, just left of the opposite corner and turn right to walk on at the perimeter. Later on, ignore a redundant stile, but then at another, a little farther on, cross to carry on with the field boundary now on your left.

Emerging onto a track Ⓑ, cross to the field opposite and continue by the left hedge. Look for a stile in the corner and carry on in the next field. Go straight ahead across a third field, aiming for a stile some 100 yards in from the left corner. Walk on towards the corner of a wood and on at its edge, passing

The Stafford to Newport Greenway

The Staffordshire Greenway is part of a much longer recreational route across the county that continues all the way to Burton upon Trent, a total of 40 miles (65km). The section here west of Stafford follows the route of the former Stafford–Shrewsbury line, which opened in 1849 and was one of very few in the country built by a canal company, the Shropshire Union. A victim of the Beeching recommendations, the railway was progressively closed from 1965, leaving only the link between Shrewsbury and Telford, although more recently there have been calls to reopen it as far as Newport.

> **Roman Roads** Much of the cross-country walk between the redundant railway and the canal follows the line of a Roman road, which ran from the settlement of Pennocrium on Watling Street, just south-west of Penkridge, up to Mediolam, modern-day Whitchurch. There is little obvious sign of it on the ground today, but the route is traced on the Ordnance Survey map of the area.

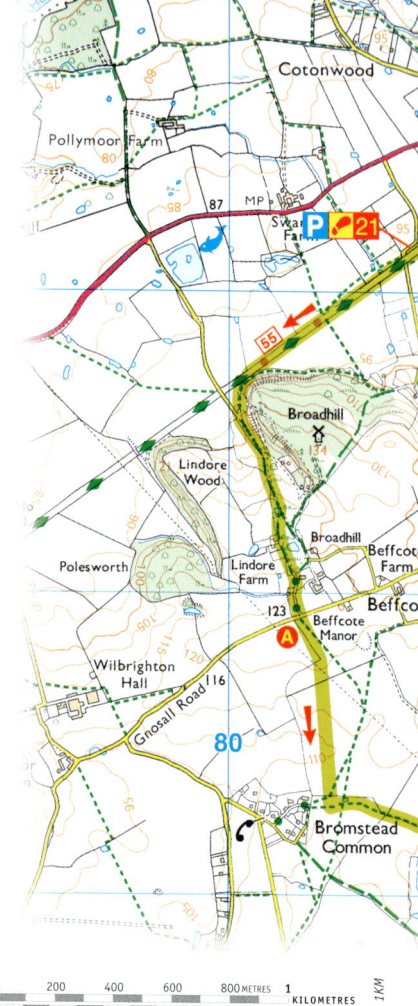

Homers Farm over to your right, and ultimately coming out onto a lane **C**.

Turn right to find a stile 50 yards along on the left. Strike out across the corner to reach a second lane. Over another stile opposite, head out to a ranch stile at the far side. Keep going forward, joining the right-hand hedge by a pond into the corner. Ignore the gate out on the right and instead take the onward hedged track, which leads to a lane **D**.

Follow it left for ½ mile (800m) to reach the Shropshire Union Canal at High Onn Wharf. Cross the bridge and drop left to the towpath. Walk away past the wharf basin and a still-impressive transhipment warehouse on the opposite bank. At the next bridge, the towpath crosses to the other bank on a roving bridge, which allowed barge horses to switch banks without having to be unhitched from the towing rope. Farther on, the canal passes through a couple of cuttings and then into Cowley Tunnel, which runs for 81 yards through sandstone at the edge of Gnosall Heath. Carry on beside the canal, passing beneath a couple of road bridges beside which are **The Boat Inn** and then **The Navigation**

The Boat Inn, Gnosall Heath

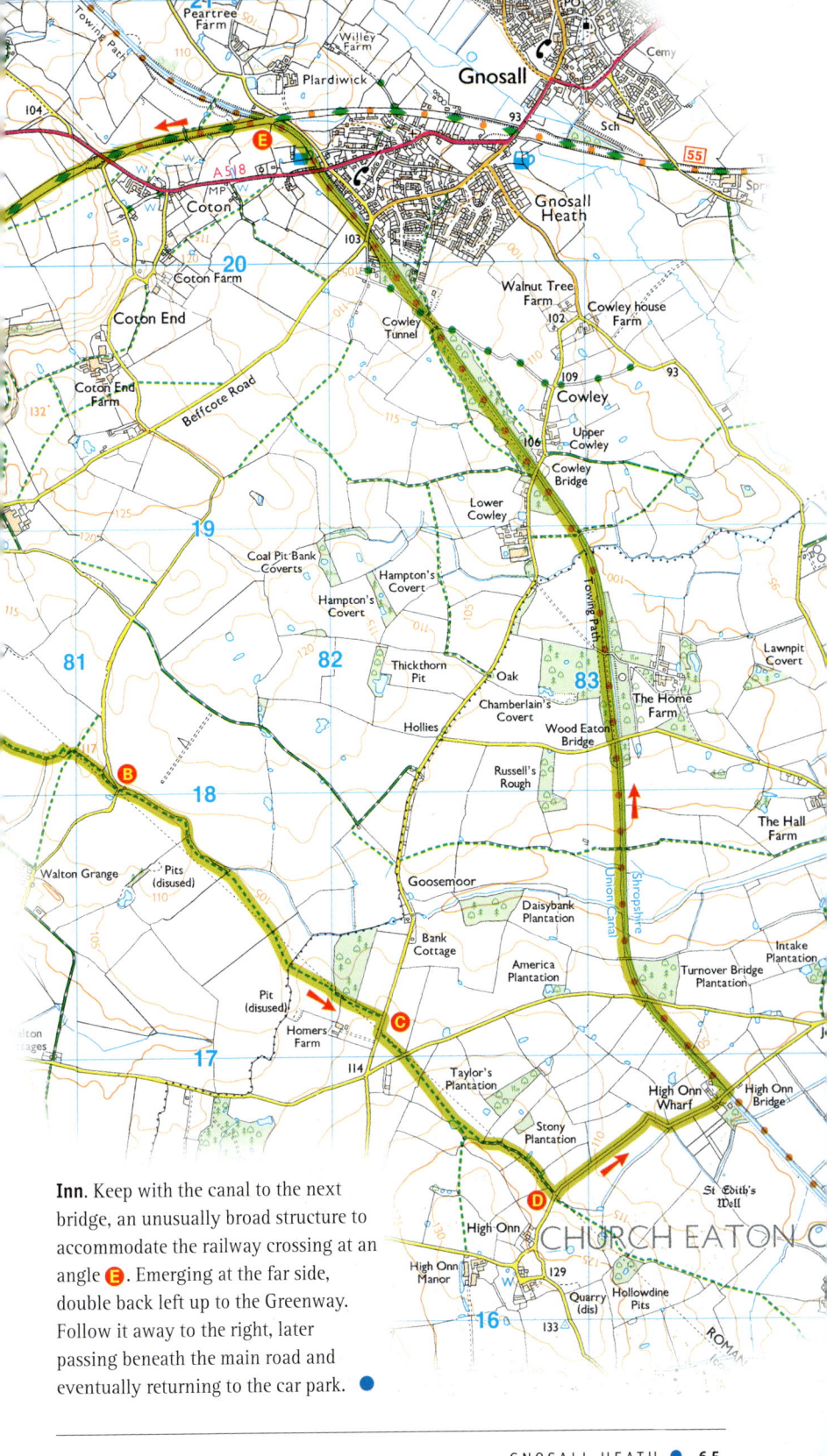

Inn. Keep with the canal to the next bridge, an unusually broad structure to accommodate the railway crossing at an angle **E**. Emerging at the far side, double back left up to the Greenway. Follow it away to the right, later passing beneath the main road and eventually returning to the car park.

walk 22

Tutbury, Hanbury and Fauld

Start: Tutbury

Distance: 7½ miles (12.1km)

Height gain: 490 feet (150m)

Approximate time: 3½ hours

Route terrain: Field and woodland paths, tracks and lanes. All well waymarked

Parking: Tutbury Mill Picnic Area, north of the town at the river bridge

OS maps: Landranger 128 (Derby & Burton upon Trent), Explorer 245 (The National Forest)

GPS waypoints:
- SK 213 293
- Ⓐ SK 192 290
- Ⓑ SK 173 278
- Ⓒ SK 182 273
- Ⓓ SK 202 281

Tutbury's spectres are widely renowned, including a former Queen who haunts the castle. This walk spirits us alongside the River Dove before climbing to secluded Hanbury, set in low hills riven by a vast crater caused when a gypsum mine exploded in the Second World War.

Walk right of the cricket pitch, through pasture to join the course of Mill Fleam on your left, a willow-lined waterway. It is the old leat to the mill, demolished in 1968. At the river, cross the sluice and follow the Dove upstream. At the ruined barn, head for the tall Scots pine beside the farm ahead. Pass left of this and walk the drive to the road. Turn right to reach the road Ⓐ into the industrial estate (look for the GPO postbox) and walk up it.

Follow this past houses and premises, shortly following the tracks of a tramroad. This linked the gypsum mines (still working) in the hills to the mainline railway; it was abandoned in 1949. Pass by the orthotics

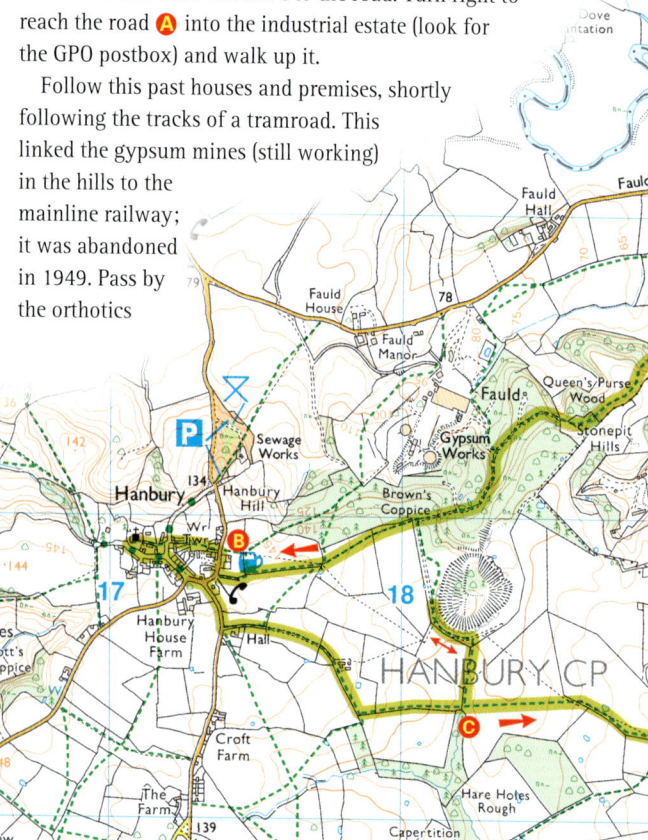

works on your right, then use the stile on the right into a field-edge path. At the far side go left up the enclosed footpath. Slip ahead right to another stile and then tackle the steep slope up the left-edge of the hollow. The path levels; waymarked posts show the way through the grassy hummocks of the Stonepit Hills, once dug for the alabaster deposits here. Alabaster was last quarried in the 1990s; in 1960 a large piece was carved to make a bath as a wedding present for Princess Margaret.

Join the wide woodland track and turn right at the T-junction. At the fork by a quarry building go left; in another 150 yards go left at the fork on a rising woodland-edge track. Where this bends sharp-right, slip left on the waymarked woodland path, which parallels a boundary fence marked by 'Danger Unexploded Bombs' warnings. Beyond wide steps the way reaches a field corner hand-gate. Rise ahead (not left) beside the woods; past the next gate drift left to another and then walk the enclosed path to the road beside **The Cock Inn** at Hanbury **B**.

Turn right. Just past the inn, go left on the waymarked path into a nearby paddock. Use the diagonally opposite

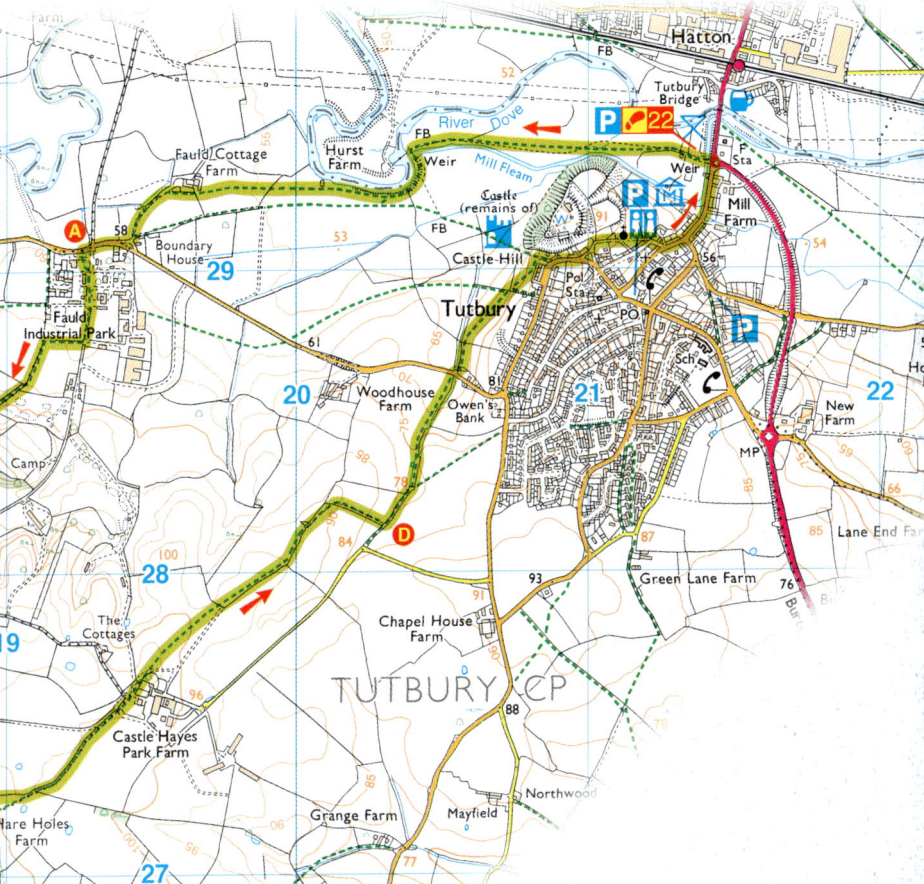

TUTBURY, HANBURY AND FAULD • 67

Tutbury Castle rises high above the River Dove

corner stile and walk the inside edge of a private house's garden to a lane. Jig left, then right over the little green to an enclosed path to St Werburgh's Church. This has possibly the oldest alabaster tomb in England, dated to the early 1300s. Below the church tower go back-left on the lane between churchyard and thatched Glebe House. Keep right at the green along Martins Lane; at the junction (in 100 yards) go left, then bend right for Burton to find the village hall. Turn left on the farm lane immediately before this. Stick with it across fields and past a farm dump. At a corner stile turn left within your field to find a hand-gate ⓒ beyond the concrete bunker.

Divert left from this gate through more hand-gates to reach the wooded crater; turn left to a memorial. This recalls Britain's largest ever explosion on 27 November 1944, detailed on the boards and memorial there. Thousands of tons of unexploded ordnance still lie buried here.

Return to the hand-gate near the bunker; then turn left over the brow. Well waymarked stiles cross a field track before turning right over a plank bridge towards a farm. Stiles and waymarks take the route left before reaching this (eyes peeled here), to pass left of a larger farm on a fringing dirt road. Be alert for the fingerposted left-turn off this, crossing fields to walk parallel to a concrete farm road; briefly join this then keep ahead as it fails left, then turn right by a hedgerow.

At a ditch and flat bridge ⓓ turn left, ditch on your right. Ignore the next bridge, presently reaching a road. Cross to the left of the cottage and head for Tutbury Castle. The path climbs to the right below the motte, gaining a lane beyond steps. Go left; then left again to the castle and nearby church. The west front is amongst the finest Norman architecture in the country, with extraordinary carvings around the door. The castle was prison to Mary Queen of Scots on several occasions before her execution in 1587: her ghost is the most renowned of several said to haunt the ruins. Make time to explore old Tutbury; the car park is downhill past the **Olde Dog & Partridge** and along Bridge Street. ●

Froghall and the Churnet Valley

walk 23

Start
Froghall Wharf

Distance
7½ miles (12.1km)

Height gain
955 feet (290m)

Approximate time
3¾ hours

Route terrain
Hilly, with several steady climbs along old railway, canal, field paths, tracks and lanes. Very muddy after heavy rain

Parking
Staffs. CC car park at Froghall Wharf, on minor road to Foxt off A52 just north of Froghall

OS maps
Landrangers 118 (Stoke-on-Trent & Macclesfield) and 119 (Buxton & Matlock), Explorers 258 (Stoke-on-Trent & Newcastle-under-Lyme) and 259 (Derby)

GPS waypoints
- SK 027 476
- Ⓐ SK 035 485
- Ⓑ SK 020 499
- Ⓒ SK 006 488
- Ⓓ SJ 999 491

The Churnet Valley's deep, wooded gorge disguises a remarkable industrial past, recalled by the canal and steam railway which both thread through this secluded rift in the Staffordshire Moorlands. This walk explores the tantalising remains, climbing to peaceful villages before encountering a hidden gem of a pub where canal and river meet in splendid isolation.

Join the rising path at the rear of the car park, pass by the cottages and walk the track for 100 yards before forking ahead right on the waymarked sunken path, an old tram road.

> **Limestone** Until the 1920s, a counterbalance-and-winch tramroad, or plateway, delivered wagons of limestone from moorland quarries at Caldon to the vast furnaces at today's car park; here it was burned before transfer to canal narrowboats for onward transport to factories and for use as fertiliser.

Today it's a lovely transect through Harston Wood Nature Reserve. Note steps on the right, climbing to an immense finger of stone, Harston Rock (a there-and-back diversion); soon after this a junction of paths is reached, just short of a deep clough.

Fork left here (waymarked Moorlands Walk), dropping down steps – you're on course if there's a foot-tunnel beneath the incline off to your right (do not use this). The path threads through to a pasture; follow the left edge to re-enter the delightful wooded valley, alive with streams, bluebells and countless birds. A couple of footbridges are crossed before a stile leads onto a steep path up the valley-side. Keep right at the smallholding, rising on a walled track to emerge into a rocky area at the edge of Foxt. Fine views of Ipstones Edge and the tracery of walled pastures that characterise the Staffordshire Moorlands hereabouts are reward for the climb. Go ahead, shortly joining a rough lane, which becomes tarred as it reaches the village road Ⓐ.

Turn right, passing above the **Fox & Goose** pub to reach St Mark's Church. Here; turn left along the 'Dead End' tarred lane, winding to its end at Shay Cottage. A waymarked path skirts the property boundary on your right, presently dropping down steps into a wooded dingle. Beyond the up-steps the way

On the Caldon Canal at Froghall

merges with a farm driveway; this becomes a tarred lane leading to the outskirts of Ipstones village. Cross the brook at the left-bend; then use the house-side steps on the right, turning right on the lane at the top. Walk by the **Sea Lion** pub and then keep left to the village centre **B**.

Turn left down Froghall Road; then right for Basford and Cheddleton, along Belmont Road. In 700 yards, at Little Stones Farm, join the second waymarked footpath left and pass through three fields. In the fourth, go half-right to a farm road at a fork; go ahead for Booths Hall Farm. Immediately over the cattle-grid use the stile, right, and head for the diagonally opposite corner of this sloping pasture and a hand-gate. Jig left, then right around the corner and walk below the line of cables and past a redundant stile; bear left at the ultimate field-end down a farm track to Glenwood House.

Turn left your side of the converted barn **C** and then right to a hand-gate

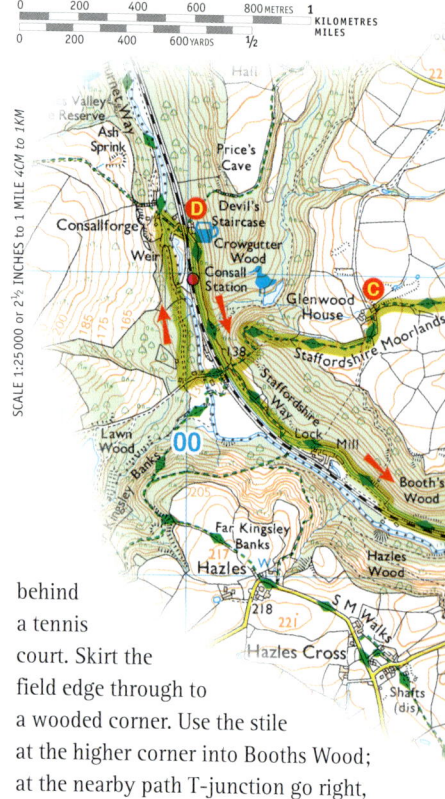

behind a tennis court. Skirt the field edge through to a wooded corner. Use the stile at the higher corner into Booths Wood; at the nearby path T-junction go right,

> **Waterways** This verdant valley once thrummed with industry, with vast limekilns burning limestone, while at Froghall the factory of Thomas Bolton was a significant copper works; wiring for spitfires was made here in the Second World War. A little farther east, works at Oakamoor produced the wire for the first Trans-Atlantic telegraph cable in the 1860s. The Caldon Canal, opened in 1811 and largely derelict by the Second World War, was one of the first to be re-opened as a recreational waterway, in 1974.

a steepening path down through this nature reserve meets a rough lane. Go ahead over bridges across the canal, railway and river; then turn right beyond the building along the rough lane to the car park at Consall Forge. Cross the river, then the canal bridge **D** to arrive at the **Black Lion Inn**, beyond the tracks of the preserved Churnet Valley Railway.

Join the towpath at Bridge 50, canal on your right, shortly passing virtually beneath Consall Station. Beyond a lock the route is swallowed by the magnificent wooded gorge of the River Churnet. Canal, railway and river share this glorious tranquil chasm all the way back to Froghall Wharf.

FROGHALL AND THE CHURNET VALLEY

walk 24

Shugborough Park and Sherbrook Valley

Start
Milford Common

Distance
7¾ miles (12.5km)

Height gain
770 feet (235m)

Approximate time
3¾ hours

Route terrain
Firm paths and tracks; towpath may be muddy

Parking
Car park off Brocton Road (Pay & Display)

OS maps
Landranger 127 (Stafford & Telford) and 128 (Derby), Explorer 244 (Cannock Chase & Chasewater)

GPS waypoints
- SJ 973 210
- Ⓐ SJ 989 213
- Ⓑ SJ 995 225
- Ⓒ SK 004 212
- Ⓓ SJ 987 200
- Ⓔ SJ 985 187
- Ⓕ SJ 981 193
- Ⓖ SJ 974 205

This delightful scenic walk on the north-western fringes of Cannock Chase features landscaped parkland, waterside meadows and open heathland, as well as the finest remaining area of traditional oakwood in the Chase. There's historic interest, too, as you pass an 18th-century mansion, cross an ancient packhorse bridge and traverse part of a disused railway built during the First World War.

From the rear of the car park walk the fringe of Milford Common towards the gatehouses to Shugborough Park. Cross the A513 and turn right to the far end of the estate wall on your left. Turn left up the bridleway and rise by the service track to the covered reservoir. Keep right of this; at the fork near the twin valve-houses slip right, down the rutted forest track. At the cross-track in 70 yards go straight ahead; this lesser grassy track heads almost straight down through the woods to reach the main road opposite a brick cottage. Turn left on the pavement; pass by the road entrance to Shugborough and look for the gates (National Trust sign) and waymarked bridleway for Great Haywood on the left in a further 250 yards Ⓐ.

Walk into the estate and advance along the tarred road. The hilltop arch commemorates Admiral George Anson, a Shugborough family member who circumnavigated the globe in the 1740s. Cross the railway and pass the car park on your left. Keep right at the fork; then left in 50 yards and remain with this roadway past Park Farm Museum and the eye-catching Tower of the Winds. Where the drive bends left towards Shugborough Hall, keep ahead on the lesser, fenced lane, leading directly to the spectacular Essex packhorse bridge across the

River Trent **B**.

Cross this and turn right along the towpath of the Trent & Mersey Canal, a tranquil, semi-wooded stretch partly paralleling the river. In about 1 mile (1.6km), at road bridge 72, pass beneath it then climb the steps, right, to the road **C**. Turn left on this to reach the A513 beyond a narrow bridge over the Trent.

Cross into the lane to Seven Springs car park. At the top-right of the parking area join the

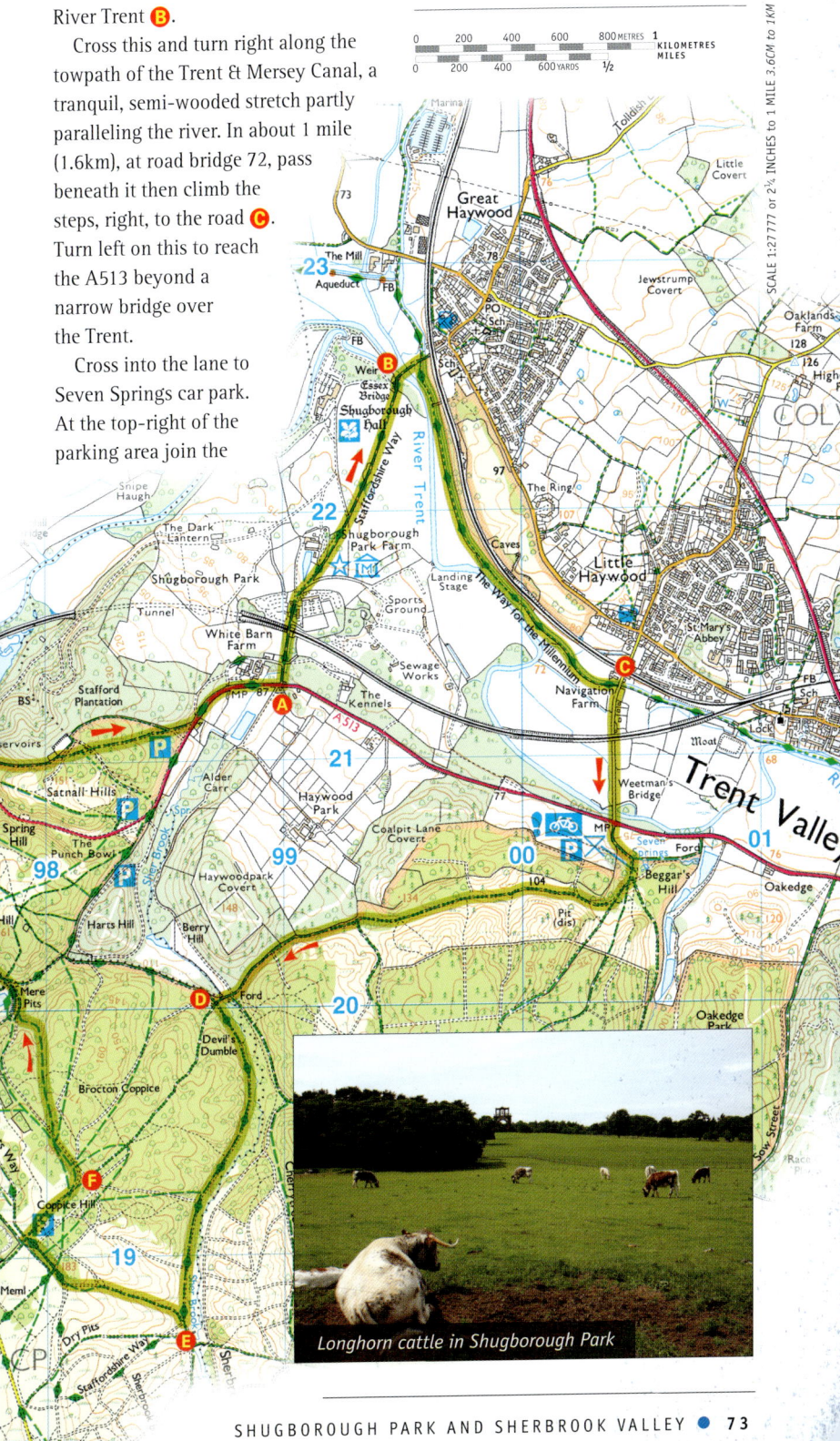

Longhorn cattle in Shugborough Park

SHUGBOROUGH PARK AND SHERBROOK VALLEY • 73

> **Cannock Forest**
>
> Cannock, or Cank, Forest originally covered a large area between Stafford in the west and Tamworth in the east, and from the Trent valley in the north to Wolverhampton and Walsall in the south. It was a royal forest, but in 1290 Edward I granted part of it to the bishops of Lichfield as their private chase. In the 16th century, ownership passed to the Paget family (later the marquises of Anglesey), who pioneered the development of the local iron industry. Demands for charcoal for iron smelting led to the felling of many of the woodlands, and much of the chase became bare heathland until the 1920s, when the Forestry Commission began large-scale conifer plantations, mostly of pine. Cannock Chase is now chiefly heath and conifer forest, but some older broadleaved woodland remains, mostly in the area of this walk.

gravelled forestry road beyond the metal barrier. In 150 yards bear right at the junction (blue arrow post) and continue to climb gently through the thin woodlands. In another 200 yards you'll pass a yellow 'caution' post on your left, recalling mining activity hereabouts decades ago. Carry on along the compacted-surface way at the foot of heather and bilberry-clad heathland, with woods on your right. At a hill-crest fork keep ahead. The route becomes a woodland way, presently lined with gnarled old oaks; simply keep on the main track ahead for one mile (occasional blue-arrow posts), finally descending to reach Stepping Stones picnic area. This sublime spot is cocooned by wooded slopes and woodland pasture **D**.

Cross the stepping stones and turn left on the wide forestry road. It's a glorious ramble upstream alongside the bubbling Sher Brook, bracketed by heathy slopes, open woodland and ridges feathered by trees. In nearly one mile (1.6km) you'll reach a grassy meadow on your left, marked by a blue-arrowed post and a major meeting of tracks **E**.

Here you should turn sharply back-right on a rising track (if you very shortly find a Staffordshire Way fingerpost you've gone too far) which soon bends left and rises up a shallowing valley to reach a T-junction at the ridgetop. There are splendid distant views from here across the heart of the managed wilderness of The Chase. The way is right, with the Heart of England Way, through a hawthorn thicket to reach a metal barrier and a car park. Turn right up the tarred lane, through the higher car park and ahead on the stony track beyond a barrier, reaching a fork in 250 yards at a small grassy area and spreading oak tree **F**.

Turn left to enter Brockton Coppice, a memorable woodland richly dressed by some of the oldest, most wizened oaks anywhere in England. The main path strikes through this bird-rich area, before descending round a sharp-left bend to a T-junction. Turn right onto an embankment above Mere Pool on your left. The bank is part of a narrow-gauge railway system - the Tackeroo Railway - built during the First War to service army training camps here. Advance with the old trackbed across a junction of ways and down a long tree-shaded cutting, at the end of which keep ahead past a red-topped post to reach a small car park **G**.

At the far end of this, fork right past wooden bollards onto a wide path which skims above a small pool off to your right. Descend to the point where a tarred driveway heads left to 'Sister Dora Home for the Elderly'. Here; bear right on the narrower path to return to the car park.

Rooks flying above Beeston Tor

Longer walks of more than 4 hours

walk 25

Above the Manifold

Start
Wetton

Distance
7¾ miles (12.5km)

Height gain
1,165 feet (355m)

Approximate time
4 hours

Route terrain
Field paths and tracks, old railway. One steep stepped descent, two modest climbs

Parking
Village car park

OS maps
Landranger 119 (Buxton & Matlock), Explorer OL24 (Peak District, White Peak)

GPS waypoints
- SK 109 551
- Ⓐ SK 098 550
- Ⓑ SK 099 541
- Ⓒ SK 124 516
- Ⓓ SK 118 535

This walk explores both the plateau and valleys of Staffordshire's beautiful White Peak. Dropping past Thor's Cave into the Manifold's deep gorge, it passes looming sentinels of limestone before climbing to an airy viewpoint at Throwley. After re-crossing the Manifold at Rushley, easy paths rise to old lead mines above Castern Wood, heralding the return to Wetton, remote amid limestone-walled pastures.

The Manifold Trail

The Manifold Trail was established in 1937 along a defunct narrow-gauge railway that sneaked through the gorge between Waterhouses and Hulme End; as such it was probably the first recreational railway footpath in England. The Leek & Manifold Valley Light Railway ran only between 1904 and 1934; its Indian-style locos and jaunty yellow carriages must have been a memorable sight. There's a railway heritage centre at Hulme End Station, 3 miles (4.8km) north of Wetton.

From the back of the car park stile, take the waymarked field path/track to the village road; here go left to a junction. Bear right for Wetton Mill and in 40 paces take the walled track left, a concessionary path to Thor's Cave. As this splays into pasture follow the signs right, around the muddy head of a sharp valley, keeping right from a hand-gate to reach Thor's Cave, a spectacular gaping hollow in a precipitous cliff.

A long series of steps drops the route steeply down to a footbridge across the River Manifold Ⓐ; in summer it may well be dry, as the rivers hereabouts are prone to flow deep underground for several months a year. Instead of water you may find a green river of vast butterbur leaves. Turn left along the tarred track beneath gorge-smothering ash woods, amongst the finest in Britain.

Beyond the car park at Weag's Bridge, use the right-hand track Ⓑ. In 500 yards, slip left over the stile onto the farm access track, continuing towards the edifice of Beeston Tor. Cross the tractor bridge where the rivers Manifold and Hamps meet. The wooden building here was a refreshment room for the old railway; the Tor was a major tourist attraction even in those days, today climbers challenge its precipitous faces. Immediately before the farmhouse, fork right up a wide track,

Looking down on the Manifold Trail

waymarked as the Manifold Trail. This climbs steadily out of the valley, revealing memorable views down the twisting course of the aptly named Manifold. Pass by an old barn and use a hand-gate shortly afterwards. From here, drift slightly left, off the failing field road and up a slight hollow up the steep pasture. If the light is right you'll make out old cultivation terraces etched across the slopes to your right.

Crest the ridge and look to your right for a hand-gate near the copse. Use this and walk the field road until it bends left. Veer off it here, heading for the left-end of the line of trees to the right of Throwley Farm. The waymarked path passes beside a farmyard reservoir, then left of the stone barn onto a tarred lane; bear left for Ilam. To your left is the gaunt skeleton of Elizabethan Throwley Old Hall, built on a medieval site; interpretation boards detail its history. Remain with this very quiet lane, drinking in the views as the Manifold escapes its gorge to merge with the River Dove just beyond distant Bunster Hill.

Cross Rushley Bridge and take the field path on the left **C**, aiming left of the distant barns (via a stile) to find a hand-gate in the corner beneath a huge ash tree. Drift right, aiming for the far end of the stone wall, from where a tarred lane rises to the imposing Casterne Hall, one of Staffordshire's finest Georgian country houses. Trace the lane around the back of the Hall; as it bends sharp-right, head left across the green to and through the field gate, picking up a wall-side field road. Memorable views now open out down into the Manifold Valley as the route eases gradually higher. After two more gateways, drift away from the wall, reaching a gate-side stone step stile just left of the far-right top field corner. Use this and head half-left to the far corner and a waymarked gate in low trees **D**.

The stony hollows here are the first signs of the lead mining that busied folk at Bincliff until the late 1800s. Use

ABOVE THE MANIFOLD • 77

> **Lost Rivers** A peculiarity of the rivers Manifold and Hamps is that, for much of the year, the riverbeds are dry, marked instead by green flushes of vegetation growing between boulders. The reason is that the limestone bedrock is locally particularly fractured and porous, allowing any water to sink beneath the surface. The rivers are still there, but flowing well underground. They re-emerge at springs and boil holes south of Rushley Bridge, where the underlying geology forces the water to surface. Only in winter will you see water flowing in the rivers on this walk.

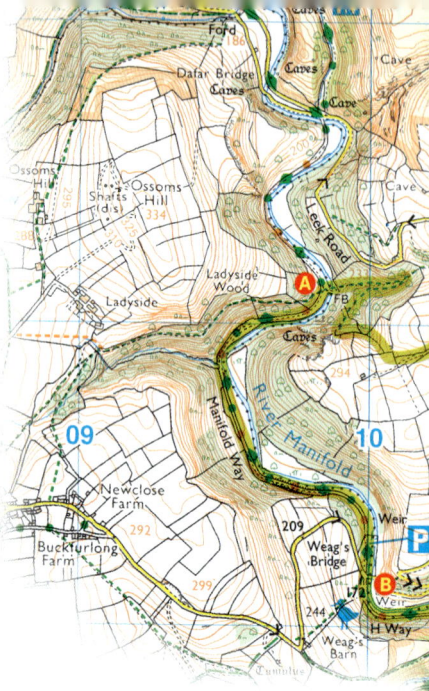

the stile ahead left and then turn right alongside the wall. The path grips the edge of the abrupt slopes here at Castern Wood Nature Reserve, home to over 240 plant species (spring cowslips and summer limestone bedstraw, orchids and scabious are notable) and 150 insects (particularly butterflies and moths). Remain with the path above a deep side valley characterised by hanging gorse and ash woods to reach a lane. Cross over, rising then to a stile right of the skyline barn. From this descend the long field past the lone tree, aiming for the distant, far bottom-right corner. Turn right on the lane to the nearby car park, perhaps repairing then to the **The Royal Oak** inn in the village centre.

Looking out from the mouth of Thor's Cave

ABOVE THE MANIFOLD 79

walk 26

Kinver and the Staffordshire & Worcestershire Canal

Start	Kinver, below Holy Austin Rock
Distance	8 miles (12.9km)
Height gain	700 feet (215m)
Approximate time	4 hours
Route terrain	Canal towpath, track, short sections on road
Parking	Roadside parking by Holy Austin Rock
OS maps	Landranger 138 (Kidderminster & Wyre Forest) and 139 (Birmingham & Wolverhampton), Explorer 219 (Wolverhampton & Dudley)
GPS waypoints	SO 836 836
Ⓐ	SO 844 835
Ⓑ	SO 849 844
Ⓒ	SO 861 865
Ⓓ	SO 834 863
Ⓔ	SO 830 843

This longer, but relatively easy walk from Kinver initially follows a particularly pleasant stretch of the Staffordshire & Worcestershire Canal. Farther on, there is rolling woodland and parkland to enjoy before a final stretch between open fields returns you to the foot of Holy Austin Rock, a fascinating example of troglodytic houses, now cared for by the National Trust.

Kinver

There has been settlement here for at least 3,500 years, the hillfort overlooking Kinver dating from the Bronze Age. The church of St Peter, standing on a hill above the town, dates from the 12th century, although tradition suggests there had been a church since the 7th century. The town developed around the High Street beside the River Stour at the end of the 13th century, where fulling mills were an early industry. Later on, the river powered iron forges and then rolling and slitting mills, which cut bars of iron into rods for making nails. The technique had been invented in Belgium, but a spot of 'industrial espionage' by Richard Foley, who held Stourton Manor, brought it here and made his fortune. Kinver's prosperity was further enhanced by the arrival of the canal in 1771 and the iron industry flourished until the end of the 19th century.

From the parking below Holy Austin Rock, walk east along the lane past a junction, towards Kinver. At a mini-roundabout at the bottom Ⓐ go left along High Street. Just

The lock below Hyde Bridge

Walking through The Million

past Jubilee Gardens, branch right along Legion Drive towards Marsh Playing Fields. Where it forks, keep right to the sports centre. Cross the car park to the playing field and pick up a path along the right boundary. Continue beside paddocks and then behind houses to a junction **B**. Turn right over the River Stour and walk on to meet the Staffordshire & Worcestershire Canal above Hyde Lock.

Follow the towpath left, rounding a bend and shortly entering Dunsley Tunnel. A little farther on, beyond a couple of bridges is Stewponey Lock, overlooked by an old toll house. Beyond that is Stourton Junction, where the Stourbridge Canal branches off to Birmingham. Keep with the main waterway, which shortly winds round a sharp left bend and over an aqueduct above the River Stour. The ongoing canal now follows the meandering course of Smestow Brook and runs hard beneath sandstone cliffs. Look out for the Devil's Den, a small cave cut into the rock, now barred by doors and partly concealed by hanging vegetation.

Carry on to Prestwood, leaving immediately before bridge (No. 34) **C** up to a track. Go left over Smestow Brook and on to a lane. Take the ongoing path opposite, which rises to another narrow lane. Follow it ahead, past Gothersley Farm. Just after, set well back behind the trees, is Gothersley Hall, once the home of Roy Wood, founding member of the 1970s band Wizzard, and where he wrote their hit single *I Wish It Could Be Christmas Every Day*. The way now degrades to a track and, passing through a barrier, enters The Million, a large, rambling wood, so called because it was planted with a million trees. Undulating pleasantly through the woodland, ignore a couple of crossing paths and eventually, over a gentle rise, meet a road. Cross to the ongoing bridleway, which leads through to the main road **D**.

Follow it ahead; there is a path along the verge until you pass a couple of houses. About 70 yards beyond, cross to a path leaving through a hedge gap. Head out across a field to the corner of a wall and then branch right, passing beneath power cables to another lane. Cross to the path opposite and strike out half-left to a stile in the end fence. Maintain direction across the corner of a second field to a gate and stile and walk out to a track opposite a pond. Enville Hall can be seen to the right, while the big house opposite is Home Farm.

Go left and keep with the ongoing track through woodland. Approaching a gate at the far side, look right to see a barred cave cut into the rock; it was an ice-house for Enville Hall. Hidden within the trees and undergrowth on the other side of the track are the remains of Sampson's Cave, a labourer's cottage

> **Devil's Den** Hidden at the water's edge by a cascade of vegetation is a cave beneath the cliffs, the Devil's Den. Not a natural feature, but excavated at the time the canal was pushed through, it served as a small boathouse for the Foleys, who lived at Prestwood House in preference to their seat at Stourton Castle. The cave is now closed off and serves as a home to bats.

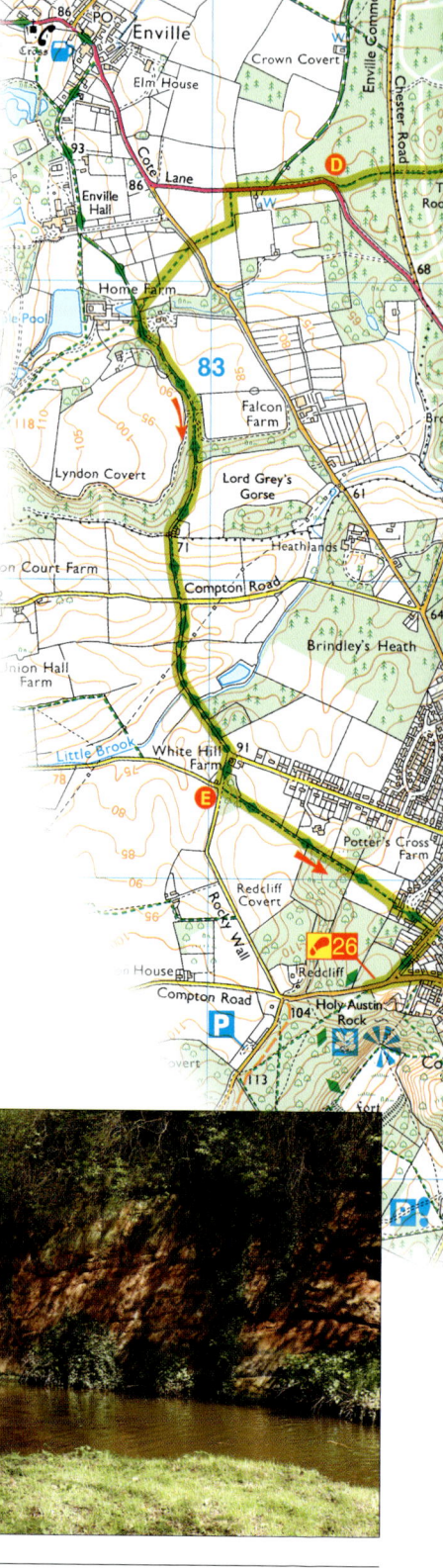

Devil's Den

82 • WALK 26

partly cut into the rock. The track carries on between fields to a lane. Cross to follow a path opposite, eventually rising to another lane. Go right to a junction **E**, there taking a footpath off on the left. Coming out onto a field, walk across toward houses, where a contained path winds out between them. Keep ahead along the street and then turn right, going right again at the end back to the parking.

KINVER AND THE STAFFORDSHIRE & WORCESTERSHIRE CANAL   83

walk 27

Mines and Caves along the Manifold

Start: Hulme End

Distance: 8¾ miles (14.1km)

Height gain: 1,440 feet (440m)

Approximate time: 5 hours

Route terrain: Paths, tracks and lane

Parking: Car park at start

OS maps: Landranger 119 (Buxton, Matlock, Bakewell & Dovedale), Explorer OL24 (The Peak District, White Peak)

GPS waypoints:
- SK 103 593
- Ⓐ SK 101 589
- Ⓑ SK 099 580
- Ⓒ SK 103 572
- Ⓓ SK 104 566
- Ⓔ SK 108 554
- Ⓕ SK 098 549
- Ⓖ SK 095 560
- Ⓗ SK 092 578

Ecton's copper mines were once the richest in the world and the massive hill rising above the River Manifold was honeycombed like a Swiss cheese by miners chasing the bountiful veins of ore. This splendid walk passes many surface remains of these formidable endeavours, returning through a section of the river's beautiful valley along the former course of a narrow gauge railway.

Exit the car park along the Manifold Track. After 250 yards, go through a gate on the left and head diagonally right across a couple of rough pastures to a bridge across the River Manifold. Emerging opposite Westside Mill Ⓐ, follow the lane right. Go round a bend and then turn off left towards Back of Ecton.

After 500 yards, just beyond a drive off right over a cattle-grid, abandon it through a waymarked gate. Climb beside the drive, maintaining the same line beyond its end. Over an intervening stile, carry on up to leave just left of a small laithe onto the lane. Turn uphill, but take a gated track off on the bend that slants back up across the flank of Ecton Hill. At the top, by the 18th-century engine house, turn through a kissing-gate and continue up the hill beside the left wall, passing

Ecton Engine House

Looking out from Back of Ecton

several capped pitheads. Through a gate higher up, branch off right and walk on, crossing a broken wall to reach a trig column that marks the summit of Ecton Hill **B**.

Head away, just east of south across open pasture, later joining a wall on your right. Over a stile, carry on past another disused mine, the way signed to Lees Farm and Wetton. Emerging onto a lane **C**, go left. At a junction, keep right and continue down the hill to the lane's ultimate end opposite a cottage **D**.

Leave through a squeeze stile on the left. Cross a stream and climb beside the right-hand wall. Stick with it as it angles up the hill to reach a couple of stiles in a corner. That on the right takes you onto the top of Wetton Hill. However, to continue the walk, go over the one ahead and bear left to a stile in the far wall. Continue on a distinct trod over the shoulder of the hill and down to a squeeze gap. Walk ahead to join a track by a small, covered reservoir, which leads down to the lane at Wetton **E**.

Bear left through the village, passing **The Royal Oak**. At the next junction, go right, passing toilets and a small car park. A path behind the car park heads upfield to emerge on the top lane. Walk left past a junction and then branch off left on a track signed as a permissive path to Thor's Cave. At the end, cross a stile on the right. Stick by the left wall, passing through a dip and up to a gate. Ahead it climbs onto a craggy viewpoint overlooking the Manifold Valley, while the path right skirts its flank to the gaping mouth of Thor's Cave **F**.

Leave along a stepped path dropping across the steep, wooded hillside. Meeting a broader trail, go left to the base of the valley, where a bridge crosses the Manifold's riverbed (usually dry in summer) to the Manifold Way on the opposite bank.

Follow it right, passing a sink where the river usually disappears below ground. Farther on, cross a bridge to a junction. Turn left beside the river as it runs beneath a steep wooded bank, re-crossing the Manifold to approach a ford at Hoo Brook; there is a footbridge just upstream. Emerging onto Wetton Road **G**, go right, over a crossroads and then a bridge across the river again. Swing left past **Wetton Mill Tea Rooms** and follow the lane to Dale Farm.

Entering the farm, turn off left on a track to Hulme End. The old valley road undulates above the river at the foot of Ecton Hill. After a mile (1.6km), look beside the lane for the gated entrance to Swainsley Mine, now flooded by a gushing stream. Across the river is an attractive conical topped dovecote by the water's edge, which belongs to Swainsley Hall on the hillside behind.

Emerging at the end through a gate ❿, go left over Ecton Bridge. Almost immediately, leave the lane through a squeeze on the right and cross a footbridge spanning a side stream. Continue briefly beside the river before turning up through a gate to rejoin the Manifold Way. Follow it right. Eventually, after crossing the river once more, the trail curves past buddle floors of the Ecton Mines, where ore was washed and dressed. Through gates, cross a lane and continue with the Manifold Way for another ¾ mile (1.2km), crossing the river a final time before ultimately returning to the car park. ●

Ecton Copper Mines

Copper has been mined on Ecton Hill since the Bronze Age, when it was discovered that the addition of a small amount of tin produced a much harder metal capable of bearing an edge. Unlike the veins of lead ore found throughout the Peak District, the deposits here of chalcopyrite (a sulphide of copper and iron) drop vertically through the hill in pipe veins, and the miners sank ever deeper shafts as they followed the deposit down. By the end of the 18th century, these were the deepest mines in Britain, reaching over 1,000 feet (305m) below the level of the river. At such depths, man and horsepower were insufficient to raise the ore to the surface and in 1788 a Boulton and Watt steam engine was installed on the hill above the main shaft. Flooding too was a problem and the water was lifted by underground hydraulic lifts and later, underground steam pumps, to flow out through soughs into the river. The ore was extremely rich, about 15% copper (1% is typical of modern mines) and generated vast profits until it became worked out during the early years of the 19th century.

Thor's Cave from the Manifold Way

86 ● WALK 27

MINES AND CAVES ALONG THE MANIFOLD 87

walk 28

Wolfscote and Biggin Dales

Start
Alstonefield

Distance
10 miles (16.1km)
Shorter version 5½ miles (8.9km)

Height gain
1,465 feet (445m).
Shorter version 870 feet (265m)

Approximate time
5½ hours. Shorter version 3 hours

Route terrain
Field and riverside paths, some lane

Parking
Several car parks in the village

OS maps
Landranger 119 (Buxton, Matlock, Bakewell & Dovedale), Explorer OL24 (The Peak District, White Peak)

GPS waypoints
- SK 131 556
- Ⓐ SK 143 562
- Ⓑ SK 142 569
- Ⓒ SK 145 587
- Ⓓ SK 152 594
- Ⓔ SK 130 584
- Ⓕ SK 126 576
- Ⓖ SK 126 564

On summer weekends, Dove Dale's popularity can make it a busy place, but for those seeking something a little quieter, Wolfscote Dale, just upstream, is an equally attractive proposition. And for those with plenty of time, a there-and-back wander into the National Nature Reserve of Biggin Dale makes this a splendid full-day expedition, especially in late spring when the hillside meadows are full of flowers. If preferred, the walk may alternatively be tackled from Biggin, rather than Alstonefield, where there is roadside parking, and both villages are blessed with a pub!

There are several car parks in Alstonefield, so make your way to the village pub – **The George**, which stands beside a small triangular green. With your back to the pub, go left and then right to head east out of the village along Lode Lane towards Lode Mill and Ashbourne. After 350 yards take a track off left past the Youth Hostel and on between fields. Later winding left and right, it ends over a stile at the lip of Wolfscote Dale Ⓐ.

Go right and then left, dropping steeply along a slight fold to Coldeaton Bridge at the bottom of the dale. Cross and head upstream beside the River Dove. A succession of weirs creates a shallow staircase of fishing pools where trout lurk in the crystal clear water. The scenery is dramatic from the start as you pass

Beyond Overdale

Biggin Dale

beneath the towering rocks of Iron Tors. Tucked beside the path in a small shelter is a ram pump that used to pump water to the pastures above. A little farther, pass Gipsy Bank Bridge, remaining on this bank to the foot of Biggin Dale **B**. *For the shorter walk, read from the next mention of* **B** *on p90.*

For the longer route, to the right, a path wanders up along its base, eventually passing into woodland higher up. Unlike the main valley, it is dry in the summer months, the stream having gone to ground. In winter however, it surfaces to run along the lower part of the dale. Less visited than Wolfscote Dale, it has a more rugged feel and is noted for its early summer wildflowers and birds. After 1¼ miles (2km), just beyond a dewpond on the left, the valley splits **C**. Swing left, going through a gate to continue up the dale. Higher up, the path forks again. This time, keep right, passing through a gate. Carry on up to the head of the dale, emerging at the top onto a lane. Walk right, soon forking left towards Biggin. You will find the **Waterloo Inn** 400 yards along on the left **D**.

The way back lies across the fields through a squeeze gate on the right, just before reaching the pub. Head straight out to a stile in the opposite boundary and then carry on by the right-hand wall. Cross a stile by the corner and now bear right to come out on a lane. Go left for 400 yards, past

> **Biggin** Like Alstonefield, Biggin sits high on the limestone plateau of the White Peak above the deep dales that characterise the area and, during the Middle Ages, was a remote grange for the Cistercian abbey at Garendon. Sheep were an important part of the economy and up to 14,000 head might be sold in a single day at the village market. Mining supplemented farming incomes and there were several small mines in the area. The village stood at a junction of old tracks, along which salt, copper and lead ore and coal were carried on pack animals and cattle and sheep driven to market, while the later turnpike between Derby and Manchester passed close by. The railway followed the same route in 1899 and after its closure the trackbed was reborn as the Tissington Trail. Biggin Dale falls from the village and is protected as a National Nature Reserve. The best time to wander through is May and June when a succession of wildflowers such as cowslip, red campion, harebells, cranesbill and several species of orchid colour the grassy slopes

By Frank i' th' Rocks Bridge

dwellings at Dalehead to find a signed gate on the right. Strike out along a developing fold, passing through a gate back into the Biggin Dale National Nature Reserve. Reaching the fork by the dew pond **C**, keep left and follow the valley back down to Wolfscote Dale **B**.

> **Frank i' th' Rocks** Supposedly named for a man who used to live there with his wife and ten children, Frank I' th' Rocks Cave can be found at the foot of the limestone crag above the bridge **E** on its western bank. The fissure was excavated in 1925 and amongst the finds were bones of animals and at least ten individuals, mostly children, as well as coins, fragments of pottery and bone and metal artefacts. They were all thought to date from the Roman-British period.

Now turn right up the valley, which is overshadowed by a succession of rocky outcrops and pinnacles above aprons of scree. After 1¼ miles (2km), at Frank i' th' Rocks Bridge **E**, cross to the other bank and take the ongoing path right. It soon turns from the river round the northern snout of Gratton Hill and meets a crossing track. Follow it left through a succession of gates, eventually rising to a sharp bend at the foot of Narrowdale Hill **F**.

Leaving the track, go ahead along a fold between the two hills. Part-way up beside the path, an old Lister stationary pump engine is another curiosity. Through a gate, keep ahead from field to field, following a wall, first on your right and then on the left until you meet a crossing track near the head of the valley. Turn right through a gate. Walk on until, just before the corner of a small wood, climb a stile on the left. Head diagonally out to the opposite corner by the wood and maintain the same line across the next two fields to a final stile out onto the lane **G**.

You can simply follow the lane back down into the village. However, to remain in the fields, follow the wall away left to a stile by a block wall shelter. Head out to another stile opposite and keep on from field to field, eventually reaching a crossing farm track. Follow it right past a farm out to a lane. Go left and left again, passing the main car park to return to a junction opposite The George.

WOLFSCOTE AND BIGGIN DALES • 91

Further Information

Walking Safety

Although the reasonably gentle countryside that is the subject of this book offers no real dangers to walkers at any time of the year, it is still advisable to take sensible precautions and follow certain well-tried guidelines.

Always take with you both warm and waterproof clothing and sufficient food and drink. Wear suitable footwear, such as strong walking boots or shoes that give a good grip over stony ground, on slippery slopes and in muddy conditions. Try to obtain a local weather forecast and bear it in mind before you start. Do not be afraid to abandon your proposed route and return to your starting point in the event of a sudden and unexpected deterioration in the weather.

All the walks described in this book will be safe to do, given due care and respect, even during the winter. Indeed, a crisp, fine winter day often provides perfect walking conditions, with firm ground underfoot and a clarity unique to this time of the year. The most difficult hazard likely to be encountered is mud, especially when walking along woodland and field paths, farm tracks and bridleways – the latter in particular can often get churned up by cyclists and horses. In summer, an additional difficulty may be narrow and overgrown paths, particularly along the edges of cultivated fields. Always ensure appropriate footwear is worn.

Walkers and the Law

The Countryside and Rights of Way Act (CRoW Act 2000) gives a public right of access in England and Wales to land mapped as open country (mountain, moor, heath and down) or registered common land. These areas are known as *open access land*, and include land around the coastline, known as *coastal margins*.

Where You Can Go
Rights of Way

Prior to the introduction of the CRoW Act, walkers could only legally access the countryside along public rights of way. These are either 'footpaths' (for walkers only) or 'bridleways' (for walkers, riders on horseback and pedal cyclists). A third category called 'Byways open to all traffic' (BOATs), is used by motorised vehicles as well as those using non-mechanised transport. Mainly they are green lanes, farm and estate roads, although occasionally they will be found crossing mountainous area.

Rights of way are marked on Ordnance Survey maps. Look for the green broken lines on the Explorer maps, or the red dashed lines on Landranger maps.

The term 'right of way' means exactly what it says. It gives a right of passage over what, for the most part, is private land. Under pre-CRoW legislation walkers were required to keep to the line of the right of way and not stray onto land on either side. If you did inadvertently wander off the right of way, either because of faulty map reading or because the route was not clearly indicated on the ground, you were technically trespassing.

Local authorities have a legal obligation to ensure that rights of way are kept clear and free of obstruction, and are signposted where they leave metalled roads. The duty of local authorities to install signposts extends to the placing of signs along a path or way, but only where the authority considers it necessary to have a signpost or waymark to assist persons unfamiliar with the locality.

CRoW Access Rights
Access Land

As well as being able to walk on existing rights of way, under CRoW legislation you have access to large areas of open land and, under further legislation, a right of coastal access, which is being implemented by Natural England, giving for the first time the right of access around all England's open coast. This includes plans for an England Coast Path (ECP) which will run for 2,795 miles (4,500 kilometres). A corresponding Wales Coast Path has been open since 2012.

Coastal access rights apply within the coastal margin (including along the ECP) unless the land falls into a category of excepted land or is subject to local restrictions, exclusions or diversions.

You can of course continue to use rights of way to cross access land, but you can lawfully leave the path and wander at will in these designated areas.

Where to Walk

Access Land is shown on Ordnance Survey Explorer maps by a light yellow tint surrounded by a pale orange border. New orange coloured 'i' symbols on the maps will show the location of permanent access information boards installed by the access authorities. Coastal Margin is shown on Ordnance Survey Explorer maps by a pink tint.

Restrictions

The right to walk on access land may lawfully be restricted by landowners, but whatever restrictions are put into place on access land they have no effect on existing rights of way, and you can continue to walk on them.

Dogs

Dogs can be taken on access land, but must be kept on leads of two metres or less between 1 March and 31 July, and at all times where they are near livestock. In addition landowners may impose a ban on all dogs from fields where lambing takes place for up to six weeks in any year. Dogs may be banned from moorland used for grouse shooting and breeding for up to five years.

General Obstructions

Obstructions can sometimes cause a problem on a walk and the most common of these is where the path across a field has been ploughed over. It is legal for a farmer to plough up a path provided that it is restored within two weeks. This does not always happen and you are faced with the dilemma of following the line of the path, even if this means treading on crops, or walking round the edge of the field. Although the latter course of action seems the most sensible, it does mean that you would be trespassing.

Other obstructions can vary from overhanging vegetation to wire fences across the path, locked gates or even a cattle feeder on the path.

Use common sense. If you can get round the obstruction without causing damage, do so. Otherwise only remove as much of the obstruction as is necessary to secure passage.

If the right of way is blocked and cannot be followed, there is a long-standing view that in such circumstances there is a right to deviate, but this cannot wholly be relied on. Although it is accepted in law that highways (and that includes rights of way) are for the public service, and if the usual track is impassable, it is for the general good that people should be entitled to pass into another line. However, this should not be taken as indicating a right to deviate whenever a way is impassable. If in doubt, retreat.

Report obstructions to the local authority and/or the Ramblers (see page 94).

Useful Organisations

Campaign to Protect Rural England
Tel. 020 7981 2800
www.cpre.org.uk

Camping and Caravanning Club
Tel. 024 7647 5426 (site bookings)
www.campingandcaravanningclub.co.uk

Cannock Chase AONB
Stafford Borough Council,
Civic Centre,
Riverside,
Stafford
ST16 3AQ
www.cannock-chase.co.uk

Campaign for National Parks
Tel. 020 7981 0890
www.cnp.org.uk

Forestry England
Central England Regional Office
Tel. 0300 067 4340
www.forestryengland.uk

National Trust
Membership and general enquiries:
Tel. 0344 800 1895
www.nationaltrust.org.uk
West Midlands Region:
Attingham Park,
Shrewsbury
SY4 4TP
Tel. 01743 708100

Natural England
Tel. 0300 060 3900
www.gov.uk/government/organisations/natural-england

Ordnance Survey
Tel. 03456 05 05 05
www.ordnancesurvey.co.uk

Peak District National Park Authority
Aldern House, Baslow Road, Bakewell
Derbyshire DE45 1AE
Tel. 01629 816200
www.peakdistrict.gov.uk

Ramblers
Tel. 020 7339 8500
www.ramblers.org.uk

Tourist information:
www.enjoystaffordshire.com

Local tourist information offices:
Lichfield: 01543 308924
Stafford: 01785 619619
Staffordshire Moorlands: 01538 395530
Stoke-on-Trent: 01782 236000
Swadlincote: 01283 222848
Tamworth: 01827 709581

Youth Hostels Association
Trevelyan House, Dimple Road,
Matlock, Derbyshire DE4 3YH
Tel. 01629 592700
www.yha.org.uk

Ordnance Survey maps of Staffordshire

Staffordshire is covered by Ordnance Survey 1:50 000 scale (1¼ inches to 1 mile or 2cm to 1km) Landranger map sheets 118, 119, 127, 128, 138 and 139. These all-purpose maps are packed with information to help you explore the area. Viewpoints, picnic sites, places of interest, caravan and camping sites are shown, as well as public rights of way information such as footpaths and bridleways.

To examine this area in more detail and especially if you are planning walks, Ordnance Survey Explorer maps at 1:25 000 scale (2½ inches to 1 mile or 4cm to 1km) are ideal. Maps covering this area are:

OL24 (The Peak District - White Peak)
218 (Wyre Forest & Kidderminster)
219 (Wolverhampton & Dudley)
220 (Birmingham)
232 (Nuneaton & Tamworth)
243 (Market Drayton)
244 (Cannock Chase & Chasewater)
245 (The National Forest, Burton upon Trent)
257 (Crewe & Nantwich)
258 (Stoke-on-Trent & Newcastle-under-Lyme)
259 (Derby)
268 (Wilmslow, Macclesfield & Congleton)

RIGHTS OF WAY
Any blockages, collapses or maintenance problems encountered on the walks in this book should be notified to the Public Rights of Way Team at the appropriate local authority:
Staffordshire
Tel. 0300 111 800
Peak District National Park
Tel. 01629 816200

Text:	Dennis and Jan Kelsall. Some text reused from the 2020 edition Pathfinder Guide Shropshire and Staffordshire, Neil Coates.
Photography:	Dennis and Jan Kelsall, Neil Coates, Brian Conduit, Nick Channer, and David Hancock. Front cover: © Dennis Kelsall
Editorial:	Ark Creative (UK) Ltd
Design:	Ark Creative (UK) Ltd

© Crown copyright / Ordnance Survey Limited, 2021
Published by Trotman Publishing Ltd under licence from Ordnance Survey Limited.
Pathfinder, Ordnance Survey, OS and the OS logos are registered trademarks of
Ordnance Survey Limited and are used under licence from Ordnance Survey Limited.
Text © Trotman Publishing Limited, 2021

This product includes mapping data licensed from Ordnance Survey
© Crown copyright and database rights (2021) OS 150002047

ISBN – 978-0-31909-205-7

While every care has been taken to ensure the accuracy of the route directions, the publishers cannot accept responsibility for errors or omissions, or for changes in details given. The countryside is not static: hedges and fences can be removed, stiles can be replaced by gates, field boundaries can alter, footpaths can be rerouted and changes in ownership can result in the closure or diversion of some concessionary paths. Also, paths that are easy and pleasant for walking in fine conditions may become slippery, muddy and difficult in wet weather, while stepping stones across rivers and streams may become impassable.

If you find an inaccuracy in either the text or maps, please contact Trotman Publishing at the address below.

First published 2021 by Trotman Publishing.

Trotman Publishing, 19-21D Charles Street, Bath, BA1 1HX

www.pathfinderwalks.co.uk

Printed in India by Replika Press Pvt. Ltd. 1/21

All rights reserved. No part of this publication may be reproduced, transmitted in any form or by any means, or stored in a retrieval system without either the prior written permission of the publisher, or in the case of reprographic reproduction a licence issued in accordance with the terms and licences issued by the CLA Ltd.

A catalogue record for this book is available from the British Library.

Front cover: The Roaches
Page 1: Looking north beyond Golden Hill

Pathfinder® Guides
Britain's best-loved walking guides

Scotland
Pathfinder Walks
- 3 ISLE OF SKYE
- 4 CAIRNGORMS
- 7 FORT WILLIAM & GLEN COE
- 19 DUMFRIES & GALLOWAY
- 23 LOCH LOMOND, THE TROSSACHS, & STIRLING
- 27 PERTHSHIRE, ANGUS & FIFE
- 30 LOCH NESS & INVERNESS
- 31 OBAN, MULL & KINTYRE
- 46 ABERDEEN & ROYAL DEESIDE
- 47 EDINBURGH, PENTLANDS & LOTHIANS
- 82 ORKNEY & SHETLAND (spring 2022)
- 83 NORTH COAST 500 & NORTHERN HIGHLANDS (spring 2022)

North of England
Pathfinder Walks
- 15 YORKSHIRE DALES
- 22 MORE LAKE DISTRICT
- 28 NORTH YORK MOORS
- 35 NORTHUMBERLAND & SCOTTISH BORDERS
- 39 DURHAM, NORTH PENNINES & TYNE AND WEAR
- 42 CHESHIRE
- 49 VALE OF YORK & YORKSHIRE WOLDS
- 53 LANCASHIRE
- 60 LAKE DISTRICT
- 63 PEAK DISTRICT
- 64 SOUTH PENNINES
- 71 THE HIGH FELLS OF LAKELAND
- 73 MORE PEAK DISTRICT

Short Walks
- 1 YORKSHIRE DALES
- 2 PEAK DISTRICT
- 3 LAKE DISTRICT
- 13 NORTH YORK MOORS

Wales
Pathfinder Walks
- 10 SNOWDONIA
- 18 BRECON BEACONS
- 34 PEMBROKESHIRE & CARMARTHENSHIRE
- 41 MID WALES
- 55 GOWER, SWANSEA & CARDIFF
- 78 ANGLESEY, LLEYN & SNOWDONIA (spring 2022)
- 79 DEE VALLEY, CLWYDIAN HILLS & NORTH EAST WALES (spring 2022)

Short Walks
- 14 SNOWDONIA
- 31 BRECON BEACONS

Heart of England
Pathfinder Walks
- 6 COTSWOLDS
- 20 SHERWOOD FOREST & THE EAST MIDLANDS
- 29 WYE VALLEY & FOREST OF DEAN
- 74 THE MALVERNS TO WARWICKSHIRE
- 80 SHROPSHIRE
- 81 STAFFORDSHIRE
- 84 BERKSHIRE, BUCKINGHAMSHIRE & OXFORDSHIRE (spring 2022)

Short Walks
- 4 COTSWOLDS
- 32 HEREFORDSHIRE & THE WYE VALLEY

East of England
Pathfinder Walks
- 44 ESSEX
- 45 NORFOLK
- 48 SUFFOLK
- 50 LINCOLNSHIRE & THE WOLDS
- 51 CAMBRIDGESHIRE & THE FENS

South West of England
Pathfinder Walks
- 1 SOUTH DEVON & DARTMOOR
- 5 CORNWALL
- 9 EXMOOR & THE QUANTOCKS
- 11 DORSET & THE JURASSIC COAST
- 26 DARTMOOR
- 68 NORTH & MID DEVON
- 69 SOUTH WEST ENGLAND'S COAST
- 76 SOMERSET & THE MENDIPS (spring 2022)
- 77 WILTSHIRE (spring 2022)

Short Walks
- 8 DARTMOOR
- 9 CORNWALL
- 21 EXMOOR
- 29 SOUTH DEVON

South East of England
Pathfinder Walks
- 8 KENT
- 12 NEW FOREST, HAMPSHIRE & SOUTH DOWNS
- 25 THAMES VALLEY & CHILTERNS
- 54 HERTFORDSHIRE & BEDFORDSHIRE
- 65 SURREY
- 66 SOUTH DOWNS NATIONAL PARK & WEST SUSSEX
- 67 SOUTH DOWNS NATIONAL PARK & EAST SUSSEX
- 72 THE HOME COUNTIES FROM LONDON BY TRAIN

Short Walks
- 23 NEW FOREST NATIONAL PARK
- 27 ISLE OF WIGHT

Practical Guide
- 75 NAVIGATION SKILLS FOR WALKERS

City Walks
- LONDON
- OXFORD
- EDINBURGH